STORY TIME
WITH GRANDMA

Revised and compiled
by
Mary Elizabeth Yoder

Cover photo by
Robert K. Monn/Monn Studios

Christian Light Publications
Harrisonburg, Virginia 22801

Copyright © 1979
Christian Light Publications, Inc.

Sixth Printing, 1996

ISBN: 0-87813-514-6

Lithographed in U.S.A.

FOREWORD

In order to raise healthy vegetables and fruits, we need knowledge, hard work, and regular care. We work the soil, plant the seeds, cultivate the ground, and pull the weeds. If not, the produce is small and unsavory. Only weeds "just grow."

Similarly, children don't "just grow" into responsible, mature adults. Good character does not just happen. God gave children parents to provide healthy experiences and examples. Furthermore, children don't "just grow" into loving God. They need to be taught who He is, and taught to love and serve Him.

Concerned parents need to share the truth of the Bible with their children. Faith in God is the basis of a strong, mature personality.

I find the stories in **Story Time With Grandma** intriguing. The scenes of yesteryear should not hinder the child's grasp of truths which the stories depict. They should inspire a child to follow the right way when he is tempted to do wrong.

I am delighted by the parents' insight and wisdom in these stories. They effectively taught by "showing." This method by far takes precedence over that of nagging. Instead of resorting only to constant stern lectures, scoldings, and punishment, the parents prepared object lessons. For example,

3

Mother actually gave Mary the doughnut "holes" after Tommy had deceived her.

A child may forget a lecture or a scolding. He may even forget the reason for being disciplined. But he will never forget an experience.

I agree with author Yoder that very early in a child's life and throughout his growing years parents need to instill character-building qualities. These Bible stories and experience stories are the seeds sown. Parents continue to cultivate the soil with more truth and examples. They pull weeds through loving, careful discipline. They allow the warmth and moisture of the Holy Spirit to give life and growth.

I recommend this book to parents interested in raising good children. I would like to read it to my grandchildren.

Ella May Miller

PREFACE

In an age when parents are being cautioned against inhibiting their offspring with strong discipline, many may be glad to find a series of stories depicting parents who had no qualms about guiding their children into paths of righteousness through appropriate discipline.

Contrary to the demand for subtle concealment of all morals in children's literature today, these stories abound in vivid, influential and conspicuous morals, the measure of a good story.

Memories of my own children's delight in these stories from the past persuade me that today's children will enjoy and benefit from them as well.

With permission from the Metropolitan Church Association and with encouragement from Simon N. Schrock, I have selected and revised these stories from *The Story Hour* series. (Recognition of book titles and known authors is given in the table of contents.)

To the Metropolitan Church Association and to others who have helped or encouraged me with this project, I am deeply grateful.

My prayer and confidence is that many little people will enjoy and be influenced by these unique stories.

Mary Elizabeth Yoder

TABLE OF CONTENTS

(From *Fireside Tales*)

(From *Sunny Hour Stories*,
by Gladys Fordham)

DOUGHNUT HOLES

Tommy Miller burst into the kitchen, letting the door bang behind him. "Oh, Mommy, I'm so hungry, I could nearly eat a-a-a elephant," he announced.

Mother paused from her doughnut rolling and smiled her understanding smile. "You may have one of the warm doughnuts in that bowl," she offered. "And take one along outside for Mary too."

"Oh, goody, thanks, Mommy," said Tommy dashing back outside with two fat doughnuts.

When Mary saw the doughnuts, a smile spread over her plump face showing her pretty dimples. "Oh, Tommy, please give me one of your doughnuts," she begged.

Right then a naughty thought popped into Tommy's mind. *Why not keep Mary's doughnut for myself? She thinks they are both mine. She'll never know it was hers.* Tommy took a big bite and wiped his mouth with the back of his hand. "No, Mary, I'm so hungry, I need both of them," he answered.

Mary's smile and her dimples disappeared like the sun going behind a cloud. "Then give me a bite," she coaxed, "just a teeny little bite, please, Tommy!"

Tommy's brown eyes seemed to be dancing with mischief. "Wait a minute and you can have the holes," he answered.

Mary was too small to realize Tommy was

playing a trick on her. Her smile and dimples were back in place and her blue eyes sparkled as she waited happily for the promised holes. When she saw the last bite of doughnut disappearing into Tommy's mouth, her eyes stopped sparkling and filled with tears. "There's none left, not one little bit," she sobbed.

"Ho, ho, ho," laughed Tommy. "You silly girl! Can't you see that the holes are still left? The holes are just air. I can't eat air and neither can you. The doughnuts are all gone, but I didn't eat the holes." Tommy slipped away still laughing at his joke.

What Tommy didn't know was that Mother had stepped out on the porch to see if there was enough wood in the woodbox to cook supper. She saw the whole thing and heard Mary crying. This was not the first time Tommy had played a mean trick on his little sister. Right there and then Mother decided to do something special for Mary.

During the afternoon the children could hear Mother beating, scraping, and whipping in the kitchen. They could smell vanilla, black walnut, and maple flavorings. But Mother would not allow them even to peep into the kitchen.

At supper time when they came into the dining room, a pretty tin box with Japanese pictures on it stood at Mary's place. Tommy's eyes shone with curiosity. "Why don't you open it, Mary?" he asked.

Mary opened the box, and inside were the dearest little doughnut cakes they had ever seen. Mother had saved the round centers of the doughnuts and covered some with pink, some with green, and some with yellow icing. Some were rolled in coconut, and some had fat walnut halves stuck on them.

"O-ooh, yum yum!" exclaimed Tommy. "Where's mine, Mother?"

"Why," said Mother, pretending to look surprised, "I'm sure I heard you giving the holes to Mary this afternoon. So I fixed them up especially for her."

Tommy looked ashamed. His cheeks and neck and ears turned red. He felt hot all over and squirmed in his chair.

"Do you think you deserve any of the little cakes after the trick you played this afternoon, Tommy?" asked Mother.

"No, Mother," Tommy answered in a very small voice.

"I want this to be a lesson you will always remember, Tommy," Mother explained. "The Bible tells us to be kind to each other. That means to little sisters too. I will not allow you to cheat Mary just because she is small. I hope you will try to treat her better."

Tommy wiggled in his chair and played with the button on his blue shirt. "Yes, Mother, I really will try," he said very soberly. Then turning to Mary he said, "I'm sorry I took your doughnut this afternoon, and I won't ever, ever do it again!"

11

When little Mary saw how sorry Tommy was for mistreating her, her blue eyes grew thoughtful. She pushed back her blond curls and brushed a crumb off her pink dress. Then she looked up at Tommy, her blue eyes sparkling. "Here," she said holding the box over to him. "I'll share my doughnut holes with you."

Mother smiled as she watched the children happily sharing and enjoying the goodies.

THE SHINY DIME

Bobby and Billy were twins. Their brown eyes sparkled with mischief. Bobby's cowlick made his brown hair stand up on the left side. Billy's cowlick made his brown hair stand up on the left side. Each of them had five freckles on his nose. Even Mother had to look twice to see which was Bobby and which was Billy. But when she gave them each an apple, she knew which was Billy, because he always crowded in and grabbed the larger one.

Mother tried hard to help Billy overcome his selfish habit, but nothing seemed to work. As for Bobby, he never seemed to mind having the smaller share of things. He cheerfully let his twin brother have anything he wanted.

As Daddy watched his sons, he felt very sorry to see Billy becoming so selfish. He tried hard to think of some way to help Billy with his problem.

One day when Daddy was looking over his coin collection, he came across an old dime. "This is it!" he said aloud, "the very thing I need."

He called the twins in from their play and said, "I wonder if there are two little boys who will clean the basement for Daddy."

Billy's sparkling eyes clouded up. "Oh, Daddy, I don't want to clean it up! I'm making a kite and it's almost finished," he complained.

Bobby's eyes kept right on sparkling. "Oh, come on, let's go ahead and do it. We can finish our kites tonight," he coaxed.

"I'm going over to Paul Snyders to see about some cabbage plants. I'll give you each a dime when the basement is finished," Daddy promised.

When he came back, the basement was spic and span, and the twins came skipping out to the car eager for their dimes.

Daddy walked to the basement and looked all around. "That's a fine job of cleaning you did," he smiled. Then he reached into his pocket, laid two dimes on his hand, and held them out to the boys. One was the old, dull one from his coin collection and the other was shiny and new.

Quick as a flash Billy pounced on the new one. Of course, the old, dull one was left for Bobby.

13

"What are you going to do with your dimes, boys? Put them in your banks?" asked Daddy.

"Um, yum," said Billy licking his lips, "I'm going to buy some striped peppermint candy canes with mine."

"I-I like candy canes too, but I think I'll buy Mother a canary for her birthday. When we were at Uncle Paul's, I heard her tell Aunt Jane that her canary's song was so cheery it made Mother feel cheerful."

"Huh!" exclaimed Billy. "One dime won't buy a canary. Will it, Daddy?"

Bobby's face fell. "Isn't it enough, Daddy?" he asked wistfully. "I did so want to buy a canary for Mother's birthday. I saw such pretty ones in Shipley's store window."

Daddy's brown eyes twinkled as though he knew a good secret. "And so you shall," he said. "I'll tell you a secret. Bring your dimes here, both of you." The twins brought their dimes, and Daddy continued, "Your dime is old, Bobby. Yours, Billy, is brand new. Because Bobby's is old and so many of that kind are lost, this one is worth fifty dollars. You see people make collections of coins, and a great many people want this particular dime. I think that will buy a canary and a cage for Mother and maybe some candy canes besides."

All the while Daddy was talking, he was smiling behind his face. That is what Bobby and Billy called it when he looked sober but the corners of his mouth twitched. Billy didn't smile behind his face. He scowled. "Aw, Daddy, my dime is hardly worth anything," he complained. "I don't think it's one bit fair for Bobby to get such a good dime! It's worth ever so much more than mine."

"Now wait a minute," said Daddy. "I gave you your choice of the dimes on purpose, Billy. Didn't you choose first? You took the shiny one and left the old one for your brother when I offered them to you."

Billy looked ashamed. "Yes, Daddy, I did," he admitted.

"And don't you think this ought to help you not to always take the best for yourself and leave the poorest of everything for Bobby?" asked Daddy.

Billy shifted from one foot to the other and looked up at Daddy. "Yes, I do," he answered seriously. "And I'll really try!"

That very afternoon Billy went to the store and bought two candy canes. When he came back, he shyly held one of them out to Bobby.

Bobby's eyes sparkled. His big smile showed his missing front tooth. "What shall I do with it?" he asked in a surprised voice.

Billy's eyes sparkled. His big smile showed *his* missing front tooth. "Eat it," he exclaimed. "You see," he continued, "we're going to be twins in everything after this—apples and dimes and candy canes and all!"

MARILYN'S SURPRISE

It happened at the tiny table in the new breakfast nook. Marilyn had eaten her egg and toast. Her milk stood untouched at her plate. "Drink your milk, Dear," said Mother, "then get ready for school."

Marilyn's dimples disappeared, and a naughty frown came to take their place. "I don't want any horrid milk," she said stubbornly. "It doesn't taste good."

"Marilyn," said Daddy from across the table, "drink your milk immediately!"

Marilyn knew that when Daddy talked to her that way she had better obey. When she was naughty, he didn't talk in his nice purry voice as he did at bedtime, when he said, "Goodnight, little Puss." No, this was different. She would have to drink that glass of milk.

Slowly she lifted the glass to her lips, took a tiny sip, made a wry face, and set it down.

"Marilyn!" said Daddy more sternly than before.

Marilyn's blue eyes snapped and her lower lip pushed out, but she picked up the glass again. "I wish there wasn't any milk in the whole world!" she declared.

Daddy looked at Mother, "All right, Mother. We'll have no more milk until Marilyn wants it," he said quietly.

When Marilyn came home from school that

afternoon, she ran into her mother's room and found her getting ready to go out and buy the groceries for supper. "Mother," she said, "may I invite Bertha for supper? She doesn't like milk either, and she would like to come to our house and eat with me."

"Why, certainly, Dear. What would you like for supper?"

Marilyn's blue eyes sparkled. "Oh, can I have anything I like? Uum, let's see, I'd like tomato soup and cocoa and toasted cheese sandwiches and French fried potatoes and ice cream. Goody, goody, I'm going to tell Bertha to come right over!"

When supper time came, Marilyn and Bertha in identical pink dresses were seated at the table with their soup plates before them waiting for tomato soup. Two surprised girls opened their blue eyes wide when the soup came. It didn't look like their favorite soup at all. It was just tomatoes with water, salt, and pepper. "Why, Mother!" cried Marilyn, "is this really tomato soup?"

"Certainly, Marilyn," answered Mother. "Of course, I couldn't put milk in it, because you don't like milk, you know. Remember Daddy promised we wouldn't have milk until you wanted it."

Marilyn looked at Bertha, then at her bowl of funny looking soup. Her eyes began to twinkle. Suddenly she giggled. "Oh, Bertha, isn't it funny, we two saying we didn't like milk? Why, it's awful good in tomato soup."

Next, Mother served the cocoa and toasted cheese sandwiches and French fried potatoes. The cocoa had no milk in it, and the sandwiches were just dry toast because Mother didn't put either butter or cheese in them.

By this time the supper wasn't funny any more. Cocoa didn't taste right without milk. It had a queer, bitter taste. Dry toast was hard to eat too.

When the ice cream came, the dishes had only a frozen bit of something yellow and sticky in them.

Marilyn tossed her blond pigtails back and looked at Daddy. "Daddy," she said, "after this I'll drink my milk without fussing, always!"

"All right, Puss. Milk for breakfast!" said Daddy in his deep, purry voice.

TEDDY'S NEW WAGON

Teddy dashed up the steps and burst into the kitchen. "Got a job, Mother!" he announced. Mother turned a hamburger in the frying pan and smoothed her hair back from her flushed face. "You have?" she said.

"Yes, and I'm going to get a shiny, new red wagon," Teddy burst out, forgetting the wagon was to be a secret.

Mother smiled and turned another hamburger. "What's the job, Son?" she asked.

"Working in Mr. Black's garden," Teddy answered importantly. "He said he'd pay as much as a man my size is worth."

"Mr. Black is a very kind man," said Mother thoughtfully. "I suppose he knows we haven't any money for red wagons during these hard times."

Teddy stuffed his tan shirt into his blue trousers and rumpled his brown hair. His eyes were serious and his thin face sober as he thought about what Mother had said. "B-but-but there'll be money for a wagon if I earn it myself," he assured himself, in a half questioning voice.

"Yes, Teddy, to be sure," Mother agreed quietly. That was all she said. Teddy's brown eyes quit sparkling as he watched her soberly. "How tired she looks!" he said to himself. Out loud he said, "Need some help, Mother?"

Mother looked up with a tired smile. "Yes, Teddy, it would help a lot if you took Sally outside and played with her. She has been hot and fussy all day."

Teddy took Sally's chubby little hand into his own strong one and led her outside. "Wide, wide," said Sally pointing at a small, very old wagon on the lawn. Teddy picked her up and carefully seated her on the old wagon. All the paint was off and the wheels wobbled and squeaked.

Sally's round face beamed with smiles and her red curls bobbed up and down. She didn't seem to mind the bumps and squeaks of the old wagon that had been Mother's when she was a little girl. "Whee-ee, Sally wide," she gurgled and squealed with such delight that Mother heard her from the kitchen.

Mother walked to the window and looked outside. A happy smile crossed her face as she watched Sally's curls bobbing up and down and saw how carefully Teddy was pulling the wagon. "Teddy's a good boy," she told herself.

Father came in to supper that night with a happy look in his tired eyes. "Mr. Black is a very kind man. He found a job for me in his factory in the city. He will take me to work every day. Thank God! I feel like a big load has dropped off my shoulders."

"Mr. Black indeed is a kind man," Mother answered softly. Teddy didn't say a word. He wanted to surprise Daddy. Besides, he was thinking of the fun he would have with his new wagon and of how Sally would like nice smooth rides on it.

Father's work began the next day. A few days later when school was out, Teddy started off for his work too, feeling like a man. He came back badly sunburned. His back and knees ached and he was very, very tired.

Mother put lotion on his sunburned face, neck, and arms. She rubbed his back with liniment. "Poor little man," she said when he was comfortably tucked into bed and fast asleep.

"He's growing up and I'm pleased with him," said Father from his easy chair. He did not say he was tired too and his back ached.

As the summer days flew by, Teddy became used to working in the garden. His face, neck, and arms were tanned a deep brown, and his back seldom grew tired anymore. Sure, there were days when the other boys in the village wanted him to play ball or go fishing with them. But Teddy stuck to his job.

At last vacation was almost over. The very next week Teddy was to get his shiny, red coaster wagon, just exactly like the one Jack and Jill O'Conner had.

Supper was over one evening and the dishes were cleared away. The family was outside, Father and Mother sitting under the maple tree and Teddy playing hide-and-seek with Sally. Only Sally didn't quite understand about hiding. Finding Teddy was fun, but when it was her turn to hide, she stood behind a shrub and said, "Here, me. See Sally here!" Teddy pretended to be surprised to find her.

Just as the moon started peeping behind the trees, Father said to Mother, "Thank God! I'm out of debt at last. But there is one thing I have so much wanted to do. You look so tired and thin. I'd hoped to send you to Aunt Mary's for a month of rest in the country. Ten more dollars would do it, but. . . ."

Teddy, who was hiding behind the tree, heard what Father said. Suddenly he forgot about hiding. He ran his fingers through his hair and made it stand up like a hay stack. Then he smoothed it down flat and put his hands deep into his pockets. *Ten dollars? Why–* he thought. The next minute he slipped into the house as quietly as a mouse. Sally toddled over to Mother and climbed into her lap.

Teddy was back with both his hands behind his back. He stood in front of Father. Trying to make his voice sound happy he said, "Which hand will you take, Daddy? Which hand?" A shiny tear started to slip out of one eye, but Teddy brushed it away quickly and smiled bravely.

Daddy looked puzzled. After thinking a bit he said, "This one," and drew out one plump hand. The closed fingers opened and something dropped into Daddy's hand.

"It's my ten dollars," said Teddy bravely, "for Mother's vacation." He smiled into Daddy's surprised face.

Mother's eyes filled with tears. She drew Teddy close and started to say something. Her voice choked and she kissed him. Then she continued gently, "Yes, Teddy, I do need a vacation, and it's very sweet of you to offer your ten dollars. But you have worked hard to earn your wagon and you shall have it. Your giving Sally rides in the wagon will keep her happy and help me a lot too. With your help and your wagon to run errands for me I can rest a lot at home. We'll have our vacation right here."

"All right, Mother," Teddy smiled as he gave her a big hug.

JUST "KEEPING QUIET"

One Monday morning Miss Jasper's usually smiling face was sober. She glanced around the schoolroom and cleared her throat. "Children," she said, "Mrs. Green reported that someone has been climbing her apple tree. You know very well those apples belong to her. Shame on the boy or girl who would steal apples from a poor widow."

Everybody, even Miss Jasper, looked at big Jim Stone. But Jim only shrugged his shoulders, laughed, and said carelessly, "Humph, don't look at me. I didn't do it. But I know who did, 'cause I saw her."

"Her?" gasped Miss Jasper. "A girl? Who was it, Jim? Tell me at once."

Jim ran his fingers through his unkempt black hair and pointed at the shy new girl sitting along the wall. "Jenny McAllister," he said slowly, looking coolly into the teacher's brown eyes.

Jenny was so surprised that she dropped her pencil. Her face grew red, then pale. She swallowed hard. Miss Jasper was watching her every move. "Jenny, is that correct?" she asked slowly.

Dorothy White's mouth had dropped

23

open. Her blue eyes blinked. "No, no! Jenny didn't do it!" she said frantically to herself. "I saw Jim Stone in the apple tree when I passed the schoolhouse on Saturday."

Jenny's chin trembled. She blinked back the tears. Too frightened to say a word she only shook her head. Miss Jasper was puzzled. Her troubled glance went from Jim to Jenny and back to Jim again. "I saw her in that tree myself," insisted Jim.

"You did not!" Dorothy shouted to herself. She was just ready to raise her hand and tell Miss Jasper, when she saw Jim's dark eyes scowling at her.

"Tell if you dare, and you'll see what happens to you," he seemed to be saying. Dorothy looked down and squirmed in her seat. What should she do? Jim was big and strong and she was afraid of what he might do if she told.

After thinking a while, Miss Jasper said, "Jenny, you may stay in at recess. I will talk to you then."

Timid little Jenny thought recess would never come. Everyone seemed to be watching her, and she had trouble with even simple arithmetic problems. When dismissal came at last, Jenny laid her head down on her arms and sobbed softly.

After a while Miss Jasper walked over to her seat. "I'm sorry about this, Jenny. If you can somehow prove where you were on Saturday at the time Mrs. Green saw someone in her apple tree, I'll believe you are innocent."

Jenny looked up eagerly. "I was at home helping my mother like I always do on Saturdays," she began. Then suddenly she remembered that Mother had sent her to the store for some groceries and that she had passed Mrs. Green's house twice. The light went out of her eyes again. "But I did go to the store for Mother. So even if she knows I wouldn't steal apples, she can't prove that I didn't take any," she admitted.

Miss Jasper looked puzzled. "Well, Jenny, I'm really sorry, but unless you can prove your innocence by Saturday I'll have to excuse you from our picnic that day," she said.

Later Jenny overheard some of the girls talking in the cloak room. "Funny about Jenny McAllister. She's such a quiet little thing. I don't believe she ever climbed a tree in her life." That was Peggy's voice.

"But Jim said he saw her and I believe him," said another girl.

"Her faded, patched clothes are proof enough that she's poor, but I didn't think she'd steal. Maybe she doesn't have enough to eat," added a third voice.

"Well, I don't trust her," announced Kay Bowswer loudly. "You won't catch me leaving anything lying around where Jenny McAllister can get it!"

Clutching at her throat, Jenny slipped out of the cloak room unnoticed.

After Jenny sobbed herself to sleep several nights, she told Mother everything. "Oh, Mother, I did so much want to go to the picnic," she sighed. Then in a choked voice she added, "But it hurts even more that Dorothy White won't even walk to and from school with me anymore."

What Jenny didn't know was that Dorothy was feeling badly too. Several times during the week she told herself, "I just can't face Jenny if she can't go to the picnic. I'm going to tell Miss Jasper about Jim." But then Jim would give her one of his looks which said, "I dare you to tell."

Jenny's mother drew her close. "I know it's hard to be blamed for something you didn't do, Dear," she sympathized. "But God knows all about it, Jenny. In Romans 8:28 He tells us that all things work together for good for those who love God. I'm sure everything is going to work out all right." Together Jenny and Mother knelt and told God everything. After that, Jenny knew that things were going to be all right even if they seemed to be all wrong.

Saturday dawned a perfect day for a picnic. Jenny smiled and sang that morning as she helped her mother around the house. The two of them were planning to eat their lunch under a tree on the lawn.

At Dorothy's house her mother looked puzzled when Dorothy came downstairs and slumped into a chair instead of hurrying to get ready for the picnic. "Aren't you feeling well,

Dorothy?" she asked.

"I have a headache," Dorothy answered. She didn't tell her mother how long she had been lying awake trying to think of some way to let Jenny go to the picnic without getting herself into trouble with Jim Stone.

"I can't enjoy the picnic knowing Jenny had to stay home," she finally decided, "I'll send word to Miss Jasper that I can't come."

After lunch when Dorothy was feeling better, Mother left her with her little brother Timmy while she did some shopping.

"Take Timmy to the sandbox in the back yard when he wakes up," Mother suggested.

Timmy's blue sparkled when Dorothy put his red sweater on him. "Timmy go out. Timmy walk," he said grasping Dorothy's slim finger with his chubby ones. She led him to the sandbox and showed him how to load his red truck with sand. Then she went to rest in the hammock. Before long she was fast asleep.

Suddenly she jumped and her eyes flew wide open. *Where's Timmy?* she wondered. He was not at the sandbox.

Raising on her elbow, she glanced to the far corner of the lot. She gasped. Timmy was up on the cistern. One board was pushed back, and he was down on his knees peering into the water!

Dorothy wanted to jump up and run, but she couldn't move. She tried to scream, but no sound came. She seemed paralyzed.

Just then Jenny McAllister darted up from somewhere. She grabbed Timmy's plump legs just as he leaned forward to get a better look into the deep water. Gently but firmly she pulled the little boy off the cistern and gathered him into her arms. She was pale and trembling as she carried him to Dorothy and put him into her arms.

"Oh, Timmy, the cistern's so deep," Dorothy sobbed. Then turning to Jenny she cried, "Oh, thank you, Jenny! How could you do it when I lied about you?"

"Lied?" exclaimed Jenny in astonishment. "That big boy lied, but not you."

"I knew all the time that Jim climbed that tree," sobbed Dorothy. "But I was scared to tell, and so I lied just by keeping quiet."

Jenny's eyes began to sparkle. "Then someone does know that I didn't do it," she cried eagerly. "You'll tell now?" she asked.

" 'Course I'll tell!" answered Dorothy, throwing her arms around Jenny. "I'll tell what a mean coward I was, and that I told a lie just by keeping quiet, and how you saved my little brother's life. And I'll be your best friend as long as I live, Jenny McAllister!"

Jenny wondered later why everyone was so good to her. The girls liked to sit with her to eat their lunches. They shared cookies, cakes, and fruits with her. Miss Jasper planned another picnic. "It's especially for Jenny to show her how sorry we are about the dreadful mistake," she explained.

28

LEARNING TO OBEY

Betty Ann brushed her blond hair back from her face and slowly, carefully counted out six and three chubby little fingers and thumbs. A satisfied smile crossed her face. "Miss Berkey was right," she told her mother. "Now I know six and three make nine, 'cause I figured it out by myself."

"That's fine," answered Mother. "It's good to want to figure things out for yourself. But then there are lots of things little girls need to do without knowing why."

"Yes, I know," said Betty Ann nodding her head wisely. "Like when you say, 'Hurry, Betty Ann,' not 'splaining that Jack has eaten all his ice cream and is about to start on mine."

Mother smiled, "Yes, Betty Ann, and bigger things too. The Bible says, 'Children, obey your parents.' There will be times when you need to obey even when I can't explain right then why I ask you to do something."

That very evening Uncle Tom and Aunt Mary came to visit. Betty Ann was in the playroom making a family of paper dolls. She was just making the mother and daddy when Mother called.

"Oh, Betty Ann! Come here, Dear."

"Why?" answered Betty Ann crossly. There was no answer and Betty Ann heard the outside door closing. "Mother probably wants me to set the table," Betty Ann reasoned.

"But there's no hurry. I'll finish cutting daddy doll's hat first."

When the cutting was finished, Betty Ann went right on coloring her doll family. She was just finishing the mother doll's blue-and-white checkered apron when she heard someone coming up the stairs. Dropping her box of crayons she ran to her mother. Mother's arms were full of laundry.

"Did you want me, Mother?" Betty Ann stammered, half ashamed. "I heard you call. But right then I was trying so hard to cut my daddy doll's hat just right. So I just kept on while it was going good and thought I'd 'splain later."

"Yes, Betty Ann. I did call. But I don't need you anymore," Mother answered soberly.

"Why, Mother, what happened?" cried Betty Ann, grabbing hold of Mother's arm.

"Only this," answered Mother, her soft brown eyes looking straight into Betty Ann's questioning blue ones. Aunt Mary and Uncle Tom stopped by on their way to Oakland. Uncle had an appointment with Doctor Malec to have new lenses put into his glasses. Then they are driving on out to the lake for a picnic supper and boat ride. They wanted to take you and Jack along."

"Oh, Mother!" cried Betty Ann, big tears rolling down her cheeks. "Why didn't you tell me?"

"I called you, Dear," said Mother sorrowfully. "Then I hurried outside to talk to Aunt

Mary."

"If I had only known!" wailed Betty Ann.

"You see, this was one of the times when I couldn't stop to explain why," answered Mother. "Uncle was afraid he'd be late for his appointment and couldn't wait another minute. He just said, 'Where's Yellow Top?' When I told him I had called you, he said, 'She must not want to go along to the lake.' Jack bounced into the car and they whirled away before you could say scat."

"From now on I won't ask why when Mother calls me. I'll obey the minute she asks me to do something, whether I know the reason or not," she promised herself.

DANNY'S BURIED TREASURE

Danny had been sick with pneumonia for a long time. Now he didn't seem to grow very strong. His cheeks stayed pale and thin. The doctor shook his head when Danny asked him about going back to school.

"Not yet, Danny. You need to grow stronger before you go to school. Getting outside, lots of fresh air and sunshine is the best medicine for you now. Right now you should be living on a farm," he explained.

So one warm day Daddy took Danny to his Uncle Jim's ranch to live until he grew stronger. His little cousin Mary Jo with the red hair and freckles came bouncing out to the car to welcome him.

Danny soon felt at home on the big ranch. He trotted after Uncle Jim and went to the village with him. One day he wandered down the street looking into the store windows while his uncle had the car in the garage to have it fixed.

When Uncle Jim came out of the garage, he found Danny with his nose pressed against the window of the pet shop, watching the tiny Scotch terriers playing inside.

Uncle Jim couldn't help smiling as he watched for a few minutes. Turning to Danny he said, "Well, Danny, are you going to stay here all day?"

Danny looked up at his uncle, his brown eyes sparkling. "Oh, Uncle Jim, they're so cute. Look at that littlest one. I wish I could have him," he said.

"They cost a great deal of money," said Uncle Jim.

"I've got a dollar. May I ask the man how much they cost?"

"Certainly, go ahead and ask him," encouraged Uncle Jim.

When Danny heard how much the littlest one cost, the sparkle in his eyes disappeared and his chin quivered with disappointment. He had little to say at supper and only nibbled at his food.

"What's the matter?" asked Mary Jo when

they were gathering eggs.

"Oh, Mary Jo, there is the cutest little Scotch terrier puppy at the pet shop, and I want him. I wish I could find a buried treasure. I'd buy the littlest one with the money."

"What's this I hear?" said a big booming voice. Danny and Mary Jo both jumped and turned to see Mr. Grant, the rancher from the big house down the road.

"Why, Danny wants to find a buried treasure so he can buy a dog," explained Mary Jo.

Mr. Grant seemed to be thinking. "Well, Sonny, people do not find buried treasure these days except in stories. But," he added, his eyes twinkling, "I believe you could find some in my garden if you were to dig for it."

Danny ran his fingers through his hair and tucked his shirt into his trousers. "Oh, may I come and dig tonight?" he asked eagerly.

"Not tonight," answered Mr. Grant with a friendly smile. "But if it's all right with your uncle you may come in the morning."

Uncle Jim smiled at Danny's eagerness. "Sure, the work, the sunshine, and the fresh air will be good for you," he said. "You have gained some weight and gotten a lot stronger already. Now if you work in the garden and get a good tan, your mother will be surprised at what ranch life is doing for you."

Early the next morning Danny was at the rancher's door. "All right, Sonny," said Mr. Grant, "I will show you where to find the buried treasure." Leading the way out to the

33

garden he continued, "See this row of beans? Under the weeds is a buried treasure. You must dig out all the weeds to find it."

Danny wondered how treasure could be buried in a bean row, but he set to work. He dug out every weed to see if there was buried treasure there.

Finally, near the end of the row his hoe struck something hard. The buried treasure! Throwing the hoe aside, Danny dropped on his hands and knees and began digging frantically. Out came a shiny little tin box. Inside was a brand new quarter!

Danny's dimples showed and his dark eyes sparkled. "Oh, I see now," he laughed as he jumped up and brushed the dirt off his knees. "Mr. Grant is paying me to weed his garden."

During those hot summer days Danny often thought the weeds grew thicker in Mr. Grant's garden than in any other garden in all the world. Sometimes his arms ached and the hoe seemed heavy. But just about the time he was ready to quit, *clink*, his hoe would strike the tin box again.

Though Mr. Grant was a strong believer in the verse which says that anyone who does not work should not eat (II Thessalonians 3:10), he did pay Danny more than he really earned. Sometimes the little boy's hoe would turn up the tin box with a fifty-cent piece or even a dollar inside. It was not long until he had enough money to buy the little Scotch terrier.

How different Danny looked on his next trip to the village with Uncle Jim! His cheeks, no longer thin and pale, were plump and ruddy. His arms, face, and neck were a deep tan. He liked to pull up his sleeves and show his big muscles.

Danny paused to press his nose against the window before he went into the store. For a minute he thought the littlest one was gone. Then he realized that the puppy had only grown bigger. "All the others are sold," said the store keeper. "But it seemed nobody wanted this little fellow."

"I'm glad they didn't," laughed Danny. Taking the puppy into his arms he hugged him tight. The puppy snuggled against him and licked his nose with his pink tongue as if to say, "I'm all yours, Danny."

As soon as they reached home, Danny ran over to show him to Mr. Grant. "Well, now, that's a fine pup," said Mr. Grant. "What's his name?"

"General Grant," said Danny gratefully, looking up into his friend's twinkling eyes. "I got him with your buried treasure, you know."

"I CAN'T"

Rain, rain, go away,
Come again another day.

Susie's little face pressed against the windowpane looked as dark and dull as the heavy gray clouds outside, and her little voice repeated the words in a weary, sing-song voice.

A smile peeped out from a snowy cap in another corner of the room. "Can't you be a little more cheery about it, dear?" asked Grandmother in her pleasant voice.

"No, Grandma, I can't," the little girl said very politely but in a tone of voice that said as plain as words, "So that's settled."

Just then big cousin Jack, who was visiting, came in. Jack was lots of fun, but just now Susie wished he had stayed in his home in Colorado. "He's so nice and jolly he makes me more miserable than ever on this horrid rainy day," she told herself.

"Come, Sue, don't be grumpy," began Jack in his joking way. "Treat me fair. I'm company, you know."

"Company!" echoed Susie scornfully. "Why you're just my big cousin Jack, that's all."

"Cousin or no cousin, I'm going to chase away the blues," laughed Jack in such a sunny way that for just a second Susie's blue eyes sparkled. She was tempted to quit frowning, but Susie crushed the feeling quickly and shoved out her lower lip.

"Let's play dolls," suggested Jack, with a comical twinkle in his eye.

"Can't. Queen Isabella fell and broke her nose off, and I won't play with those horrid little princesses."

"Help me make a kite. We will fly it tomorrow."

"Can't, you silly boy. Girls don't know how."

"Have a tea party and invite me. I will be the king and you can take Queen Isabella's place. It doesn't make any difference about the nose. Pug-noses are as good as—"

"Can't!" cried Susie, ready to laugh, but determined that she wouldn't. "I asked Mother, and she said I must do my homework first."

"Do it now."

"What? Get the problems? Can't. Got all but the last one. Tried and tried and it won't come out right. Miss Benson didn't explain it."

"Maybe we can do it together."

For a moment Susie eyed Jack scornfully. Then she gave in. "Can we really? Then come and help me."

For the next fifteen minutes Susie's golden head and Jack's fine, dark, manly one bent close together over the old slate. Jack explained the problem very slowly and patiently.

"I can't," said the little girl, fighting back

the tears that were rolling down over her blue dress. "I'm just too dumb."

"Don't say that, Sue. 'Course you can't if you say so."

Susie's blue eyes opened wide. "Do you mean I can do it if I say I can?"

"Say, I'll try," said Jack soberly.

With a very sober face Susie said the words as if she were promising to go to prison for the rest of her life.

"Why!" she cried a moment later, perfectly astonished. "Jack, have I got it right? Is that the answer?"

"It surely is," cried Jack, throwing the slate up in the air and catching it just in time to keep it from bumping Susie's head.

Twirling her slate pencil thoughtfully Susie said, "And I only said, *I'll try*. Is that why I got it right, Jack?"

Tall cousin Jack looked down at Susie with a merry twinkle in his mischievous dark eyes. "Maybe so," he replied soberly.

"And when I said *I can't*, I just couldn't," said Susie briskly.

"It was really because your attitude had changed, Susie," Jack added seriously. "When you made up your mind to really try instead of saying, *I can't*, you got the answer."

WHEN THE CLOCK
FORGOT

Benny Burton ripped the wrapping paper off his birthday gift and tore the box open. His brown eyes sparkled, "Oh, thank you! It's just what I need. Now I can set my alarm clock, and you won't ever have to call me again!" Benny stroked the shiny chrome on his clock and carefully carried it upstairs to his room. He wound it, set the time at 7:45, and hurried downstairs to get ready for school.

One afternoon he rushed home from school like a small whirlwind and ran all through the house calling his mother. He found her on the back porch capping strawberries for the shortcake for supper.

"Mother," gasped Benny, "Gerald Davis is going fishing at the Big Rocks early in the morning, and I want to go with him. May I, Mother?"

Mother got up, washed her hands, and dried them slowly. "Wait until Father comes home and ask him," she answered.

Benny skipped out to the front porch to wait for Father. When the car came into sight, he dashed down to the drive.

"Daddy, Daddy, may I go fishing down at the Big Rocks with Gerald tomorrow?"

Mr. Burton's eyes were sober, but they twinkled as though he knew something he wasn't going to tell. "I'm sorry, Son," he answered slowly. "But I can't let you go fishing with Gerald tomorrow."

Benny's eyes snapped and a frown crossed his usually sunny face. "Why not?" he asked very impatiently. "Gerald's father is going, and he will take good care of me."

"I can't tell you why just now, except that there may be other plans for tomorrow. So please forget it for tonight," replied Father.

Benny walked back to the house with the corners of his mouth turned down and his jaw jutting forward. He looked gloomy at the supper table. Then suddenly as he dipped ice cream on his apple pie, he thought of a plan. His alarm clock! "I know. I can wind it up and set it for four o'clock. I know I'll hear the little 'ting' it always makes when it is wound even if the alarm lever is set at silent."

Benny began to look cheerful again. Mother saw the mischief in his eyes and wondered what was on his mind.

At bedtime Benny was too excited to be tired. He wound his clock and set the alarm for four o'clock. He laid out his tan shirt and corduroy pants all ready to jump into them at four o'clock. Then he jumped into bed.

The sun was shining into his room when he awoke the next morning. His father was bending over his bed saying, "Come, Benny. Boys that intend to go fishing with Mother and Daddy at Grandpa's private lake must get up and hurry down to breakfast."

Benny sat straight up and rubbed his eyes.

40

He shook his sandy hair back from his forehead. He tumbled out of bed and scrambled into his clothes. Then he remembered the fishing trip he had planned with Gerald. *I wonder why I didn't hear the little "ting" of the alarm*, he thought. He picked up the clock and looked it over carefully. The luminous hands were moving around its black face as usual. It seemed all right, but he found that in his excitement the night before he had forgotten to wind the alarm.

Benny looked so sober when he came down to breakfast that Mother looked at him anxiously. "What's the matter, Benny? Don't you feel well?"

"Yes, Mother, I'm all right," stammered Benny. "But I—don't think—I can go—to Grandpa's." Then he told how he had planned to get up early and sneak away to Gerald's and go fishing. "So you see I don't deserve to go to Grandpa's," he finished.

"No, Son, you don't deserve to go," said Daddy. "But since you have been so frank in telling us about it, I think it would be all right for you to go anyway, don't you, Mother?"

Mother smiled and kissed Benny, which he knew meant *yes*.

Benny rushed upstairs to get his cap and fishing rod. He picked up his alarm clock, looked at it lovingly and said, "I'm so glad you forgot to wake me when I told you to. You're a good clock, Big Ben, and I'm going to be a good Little Ben. Good-by!"

41

THE CUSTARD TRIPLETS

The Roland Triplets were the three liveliest children on Baker Street. They ran errands so cheerfully that Daddy called them "Hop, Skip, and Jump."

"Of course, we have real names, nice names," Melvin the triplet boy explained. "But you see, Daddy can't always stop to call us Mary, Melba and Melvin, so he just says 'Hop, Skip, and Jump' for short. Sometimes when he's in a real big hurry, he calls us the 'Custard Triplets,' 'cause we all just love custard."

One sunny afternoon when the triplets were playing, Mary squinted her blue eyes and said, "I wish I had a whole big kettle full of custard."

"Huh!" cried Melvin blinking. "I'd want more than a kettle full. I'd want a whole big washtub filled clear to the top with butterscotch custard!"

"Oho!" laughed his sisters. "You could never eat so much. And p'raps you'd fall in and drown!" They all threw back their tousled heads and laughed as they thought of how funny Melvin would look trying to swim in custard.

"Well," said Melba, hopping on one foot. "I'm afraid there's no use wishing, so let's play."

"Yes, let's play hide-and-seek," chimed in Melvin and Mary.

Hop, skip, jump, they raced to the back porch where Mother was making pickles. Swoosh! Suddenly the Custard Triplets dashed by and nearly knocked her over. Mother straightened up and pushed her glasses back where they belonged. "You'd better run out to the springhouse to play," she said. "I'm much too busy to have you racing in and out of the house this afternoon."

"All right," agreed Hop, Skip, and Jump. They turned and ran down the steps and out to the springhouse. The game of hide-and-seek went on with the springhouse door as base. Then one time when Melvin was "It," Mary could not be found anywhere.

"Where can she be?" said Melvin. "I've looked everywhere, and I can't find her." He walked away a few steps. Suddenly the springhouse door clicked open. Mary put her hand on the outside and said, "Home free."

"Oh, Mary, what a grand place to hide! How'd you ever get in?" asked the others.

"Through the window," she answered, looking very queer. "And—and I saw something in there."

"Wh-what was it?" asked Melvin in a whisper. "A— ghost?"

"Course not!" said Mary scornfully. "You know there aren't any ghosts." Leading the way into the springhouse she pointed, "Look at that!" There on the shelf by the water trough stood a kettleful of custard, cooling.

"O-o-h!" exclaimed Melba. "It's the kettleful of custard you wanted, Mary! Do you suppose it's cooling for supper?"

"Maybe it is," answered Mary. "But I'm hungry right now. I wish I could have some right away."

"Let's taste it," suggested Melvin.

"I'm afraid if we tasted it, we'd keep on eating until a lot of it was gone, and Mother would know."

"Well, if we're going to taste it we'd better do it now. Mother may come and get it soon," reasoned Melvin.

Away they ran to the playhouse and returned with three old cups and spoons. Melvin watched as Mary carefully filled the cups with the thick yellow custard. "Um yum, it's my favorite—butterscotch," he cheered. Then the triplets sneaked back to the playhouse. Just as they got inside, they saw Mother go to the springhouse to get the custard.

"Wow, I'm glad Daddy built this playhouse for us to play in," exclaimed Melba. "It's the best place to eat our custard so Mother doesn't catch us."

"It sure is," agreed Mary. "Let's have a custard party and invite all of our dolls."

It took quite a while to get Sally Anne, Susie Jane, Sammy John, Becky, Betty, and Billy dolls to sit up properly at the tiny table. Becky, Betty, and Billy just slumped down and their heads dangled onto the table. Finally the children took the dolls into their

44

laps. They bowed their heads and said together, "God is great and God is good. And we thank Him for our food. Amen."

"Now," planned Mary, "we must all take a bite together. When Mother finds out we've been into something, she always says, 'Who started this?' If we all take a bite at the same time, we can each say, 'I didn't!' "

Mary filled Sally Ann and Betty's spoons with custard. Melba filled Susie Jane and Becky's spoons, and Melvin filled Sammy John and Billy's spoons. "All right, now each of us will get a huge spoonful, and I'll count to three," planned Melvin. "When I say *go*, everyone take your bite."

Three more spoons were heaped full of custard. Melvin slowly counted, "One, two, three—*go*!" and promptly filled his mouth with custard.

And then such a sputtering and choking you never heard. Becky, Betty, and Billy were tossed to the floor as the triplets jumped up.

"Oh it burns, it burns!" cried Melba, wiping tears from her eyes.

"What is it? What is it?" cried Melvin running outside to spit it out.

"It's mustard!" cried Mary. "Mother made it for the pickles she's canning. Why didn't we think of that before?"

In the kitchen Mother was measuring mustard and mixing pickles to put in jars for next winter. "Well, this is strange," she said out loud. "I'm sure I made enough mustard for these pickles, and there are three cupfuls gone."

Just then she heard a clatter of running feet outside. The triplets came dashing into the kitchen screaming, "It burns! It burns! Water, water! Please give us drinks quick!"

Mother dropped her mixing spoon, and quickly got three glasses while Melvin ran to the pump and began yanking the handle up and down.

Mother's eyes were puzzled as she watched Hop, Skip, and Jump drinking big gulps of water. "What have you three been into?" she asked. "What burns? Why are you so very thirsty?"

Six blue eyes looked down at the woven rug and three plump faces grew rosy.

"Mary found it," stammered Melba.

"We—we thought it was custard," added Melvin. "We were going to have a custard party."

"And we all tasted it together and it was horrid mustard!" explained Mary.

Mother's eyes began to twinkle and the corners of her mouth twitched. "So that's where my mustard went!" she exclaimed. She wiped her hands on her apron and smoothed back her hair. Just then Daddy came in.

He looked at Mother and the triplets. "What's going on?" he asked. "You look as though you don't know whether to laugh or cry."

46

Mother, with the help of Melba, Mary, and Melvin soon told him the whole story. Now Daddy's eyes twinkled and the corners of his mouth twitched. "I'm sure my Custard Triplets have learned a lesson," he chuckled, "and they will never try to sneak custard from Mother again."

"No! No! No!" chorused the triplets.

EGGS

Charles passed Mr. Pratt's window for the twenty-third time that week to look at the bicycle inside. There it stood gleaming in its red paint and silver trimmings. He tucked his blue shirt into his denims and looked back longingly once more. "No, I can never have it, so there's no use wanting it," he said aloud. He walked on toward home with a lump in his throat that felt as big as a football.

Turning down his own street Charles saw his mother on the porch waving a letter in her hand. Her eyes were sparkling as he dashed up the steps. "Here's a letter from Aunt Martha," she smiled. "She wants to know if we know of a boy who would like to help Uncle Fred with the chores and take care of the chickens this summer."

The football vanished from Charles's throat. His eyes sparkled. "Oh! She means me! She means me! Doesn't she, Mommy?" he shouted, clapping his hands and hopping around on first one foot and then the other.

Charles was very busy the next few days. He asked Daddy dozens of questions. He even asked which cows gave buttermilk and if they grew eggs on eggplant!"

One night after Charles had gone to bed, Daddy chuckled his quiet chuckle. "Our son really needs to go to the farm and find out things for himself," he told Mother.

Charles packed his suitcase several times trying to decide just what he would need on the farm. At last the day came when Uncle Fred and Aunt Martha came to the city to pick him up.

When they arrived at the farm, Pal, the big golden collie came to meet them barking joyously. "Hi, old fellow, we're back," said Uncle Fred in his deep, friendly voice. Then noticing Charles still in the car with the door closed he said, "Pal's all right. Come and say hello to him, Charles."

Slowly Charles climbed out and walked over to Pal, who was wagging his tail furiously. "Hello, Pal," Charles said shyly. To his surprise the dog lifted his white front paw to have it shaken. Charles shook the paw, looked into Pal's friendly brown eyes, and the two were fast friends.

With Pal at his heels, his beautiful bushy tail waving in the breeze, Charles soon explored every nook and corner on the farm.

Every day he fed the chickens, gathered the eggs, helped his uncle with the chores, and hoed in the garden.

One rainy morning Charles couldn't hoe, so he went to the barn to play. "Let's pretend we found an Indian's cave with hidden treasure in it. You can help me find the treasure," he told Pal.

"Now I must look carefully," he whispered to the dog. Pal pricked his ears and sniffed the air as though he was sure they would find something, and Charles prowled among the grain sacks, poking behind them with an old broom handle.

Suddenly there was a rustling sound. Charles jumped back just in time as something darted by and rumpled his thick brown hair. "Squawk! squawk! squawk!" clucked a fat white hen as she rushed between grain sacks on her way outside into the rain.

"Ooo! that was close!" exclaimed Charles, running his fingers through his rumpled hair. "And it scared me too. Why didn't you tell me an Indian was hiding behind that rock?" he asked Pal. Pal's eyes shone with excitement and his tail wagged eagerly. He was waiting for Charles to tell him to chase the hen.

Now over his fright, Charles peeped behind the sack from which the hen had come. There was a nest of twelve pearly white eggs. "Oh," he exclaimed. "Pearls! I've found the treasure. Won't Aunt Martha be surprised when I bring her twelve extra eggs?" He began to gather eggs as he spoke.

Suddenly he remembered the bicycle in Mr. Pratt's window. He stopped to think. "Pal," he said at last, "I do want a bicycle. Why don't I save these eggs? I can take a few out of the nests every day and sell them. By the end of the summer I'd have enough money to buy a bicycle. I can hide the eggs in the hay loft and Aunt Martha will never know."

Charles filled his pockets with eggs. He was just ready to climb to the hayloft when he heard Aunt Martha calling his name. He didn't take time to take the eggs out of his pockets. Dashing outside into the rain, he ran to the house just as he was, his overalls bulging out in funny lumps.

"Charles," said Aunt Martha, "will you please sit down and shell these peas for dinner?"

Charles liked peas, especially when they were fresh out of the garden. "Sure, Aunt Martha," he replied trying to make his voice sound as though nothing was wrong. He took the pan and climbed onto the high kitchen stool.

Sitting down crowded the eggs and crunched them together in his pockets. Suddenly, "Poof, crack, crackle!" The noise startled Aunt Martha and Charles. Soon a horrible odor filled the kitchen, and a gooey yellow mess began soaking through Charles' overalls and dripping on the floor.

"Why, Charles!" exclaimed Aunt Martha, her kind brown eyes filled with dismay, "What is it?"

Charles felt hot. His face grew red. Slowly, with downcast eyes he told Aunt Martha the whole story. As he spoke, not only his face but his neck and ears grew red. He felt as though they were burning.

Aunt Martha smoothed back her hair and turned her face to hide a smile. She tried hard to look sober but her eyes twinkled as she looked at the funny lumps sticking out on Charles's overalls and the mess dripping on the floor. Holding her hand over her nose she explained, "That hen must have stolen a nest to hatch herself a family of baby chicks, but the eggs were not fertilized and they are rotten. I'm sure you will never try anything like that again, will you, Charles?" she added.

"Oh, no!" Charles replied eagerly. "Not even to get the best bicycle in the whole world!"

"Now we must get you and the kitchen cleaned up before Uncle Fred comes home from town," she said hurrying upstairs to get his clean clothes.

By the time Uncle Fred came home, Charles and the kitchen were both shining and the house smelled only of boiling peas. But when Uncle came in, Charles cleared his throat, coughed, and then quickly told him the whole story. "I'm sorry, Uncle Fred, and I won't ever, ever do anything like that again!"

Uncle Fred pulled his red bandana out of his pocket and wiped sweat from his face to hide his big smile. "I believe you, Son," he said, his blue eyes twinkling and his mouth twitching as he thought of the rotten eggs. "The next best thing to doing right," he added, "is to admit it if you've done wrong."

"Charles," said Uncle Fred a few weeks later, "I brought home a piece of machinery this afternoon. It's in the truck. Will you get it and put it away, please? I think you can manage it."

"Yes, sir. Sure, I'll do it now," he answered.

Very soon a radiant little boy was back in the kitchen, dragging a bicycle with him. "Oh Uncle Fred! Aunt Martha!" he gasped. "Oh, what a beauty! It's the very one I wanted. Just like the one in Mr. Pratt's store!"

"I bought it for a good farmer boy at my house. Do you like it?" asked Uncle Fred with twinkling eyes.

"Do I! Just look! Streamlined, built-in headlight, real speedometer, built-in tool box, and—oh, everything is just grand!" he said, getting things all mixed up in his excitement.

Then he looked up soberly. "But I don't deserve it, Aunt Martha," he almost whispered.

"We don't deserve a great many things our Heavenly Father gives us," she said softly, "but He is good and kind to us anyway."

"BORROWED" SKATES

"Evan s-says I can b-borrow his skates to-night," stammered Jerry Allen. "He went to Wallace King's party, you know."

"Right here, Jerry," said Mrs. Hall, opening the clothes closet at the entry, and pointing to the skates hanging on the wall.

Jerry took the skates and slung them over his shoulder. "Thank you, ma'am," he said. "I'll be real careful with them, Mrs. Hall."

"You're more than welcome, Jerry," said Mrs. Hall with a smile. "Evan is glad to have his friends borrow his skates, and I am happy to have him share them."

"Who was at the door just now?" asked Mr. Hall as Mrs. Hall settled down to finish some sewing.

"Jerry Allen," answered Mrs. Hall. "He wanted to borrow Evan's skates. The boys have been borrowing them all winter."

"Well, now, that's generous of Sonny," beamed Mr. Hall over his newspaper. "We ought to do something especially nice for him, Mother, so he'll know how we feel about it."

"Have you anything in mind?" asked Mrs. Hall.

"Well, he's always talking about Burton Hampstead's Canadian hockey skates. Those skates are expensive, but I think he deserves them, and it would do him good to know how we appreciate his unselfishness."

Mr. Hall buried himself in his newspaper

again. Evan's mother smiled. She knew that Evan would have his reward.

At nine o'clock Evan came home from the party. Before going to bed he peeped into the hall closet.

"If you're looking for your skates, Jerry Allen came for them," said Mother. Then lowering her voice she added, "You don't know how glad Daddy and I are to find we have such an unselfish boy!"

Evan squirmed, his cheeks grew red, and he rumpled his brown hair. "Aw, that's nothing," he stammered. "It's just a little thing."

Mother was puzzled by his uneasiness and his answer. Then she decided he was embarrassed by her praising him and thought no more about it.

Sunday dawned crisp, cold and sunny, a perfect day for skating. A perfect day too for walking to Sunday school!

Evan dressed in his Sunday best, his hair combed neatly against his head. "I'm going early for Sunday school so I don't need to hurry," he told Mother.

Mother went about the house, her brown eyes sparkling with a happy look on her face. "Did you ever see a better boy?" she exclaimed to Daddy as they were getting ready for church.

And what was Evan doing meantime?

Two blocks from the house he met Jerry Allen. "Where are they?" he asked, as they

54

turned away from the street which would have taken them to Sunday school and started toward the river.

"Under the willows down by Widow Hanson's house," answered Jerry. "Mine are there too, and we can go skating right in front of her house. It's the best spot on the river."

The ice, the day, everything was perfect except the feeling in Evan's heart. Even that was not as bad as it had been the first few times. All winter Evan had been having friends borrow his skates on Saturday night so he might use them himself the next morning during Sunday school.

This is a safe place, Evan mused as he cut shining figure eights on the glassy surface. *Mother'n Dad would never come down here on Sunday. I s'pose it's about time to go home though, or they'll find out I haven't been to Sunday school.* "What time is it, Jerry?" he called to his chum.

Jerry was just pulling out his pocket watch when a long blue car turned by the bend in the road. Evan knew that car! "Oh-h," he gulped. "It's Mother and Dad. Whatever are they doing here?"

The car slowed down and came to a stop. "Get in, Evan," commanded a stern voice. Evan made a straight line toward the bank and scrambled into the back seat, skates and all.

"Mother," said Daddy, "you go in and see how sick Mrs. Hanson is, and Evan and I will have a talk here in the car."

"Now, Son," began Daddy, when Mother had gone into the little house, "have you anything to say?"

Evan squirmed in the seat and stared hard at the floor. "N-no, sir," answered a shaky voice.

"Is this why you have been so willing to let the boys borrow your skates on Saturday nights, Son?" asked Daddy.

"Y-Y-Yes. But, Daddy, how did you find out?" stammered Evan.

"Never mind how we found out, Son," answered Daddy. "Remember that verse in Numbers 32:23? It says, 'Be sure your sin will find you out,' and so it has." Then he added seriously, "Do you know what this is going to cost you, Evan?"

Evan looked up quickly, his brown eyes fearful. "Cost me, Daddy?" he asked anxiously.

"Last night," said Daddy slowly, with tears in his kind blue eyes, "Mother and I thought we had the most unselfish boy in town. And we were so pleased that we decided to buy him a pair of Canadian hockey skates like Burton Hampstead's. But after this, well, you've not only lost the new skates but your old skates will have to be put away for two weeks."

A very sober boy rode home in the back seat of the blue car. "Canadian hockey skates, like Burton Hampstead's." The words rang dolefully in his ears and a salty tear darted down over his heavy blue coat.

After that, Evan was always in his place, on time, at Sunday school.

A ROBIN FOR A DAY

"Time to do the dishes, Dear. Mother wants to get started with the baking," called Mother one Saturday morning.

Phyllis's blue eyes clouded and her lower lip pushed out. "Oh, dear," she mumbled throwing down her book. "I wish I wouldn't have to work all the time!"

"Phyllis," said Mother sternly, "what did you say?"

"Nothing," she said stubbornly. Then she burst out, "Anyway, I wish I was a robin. They don't have to work. They just fly around and have a good time."

"Hm-m" said Mother, "I've a good mind to let you live for one day just like a robin does. You'll have to wait till next Saturday, though. It's too late to start today. During the week you will have to go to school, but next Saturday you shall be a robin. You may even wear your brown dress with the red collar."

It was nine o'clock before Phyllis finally finished the dishes. Then she went about pouting and flicking the dustcloth carelessly over the furniture.

All week she waited eagerly for Saturday. She would be a robin then and have nothing to do all day!

On Friday night Mother said, "I think it would be wise for you to start being a robin tonight. Of course, you won't have to help with the dishes. But the sun is going down, so you'll have to go right to bed."

"But Mother," began Phyllis dismayed, "it's not near bed time. It's only seven o'clock!"

"I know, Dear, but robins go to bed by the sun, not by the clock," Mother answered firmly. And Phyllis went to bed.

Early in the morning, very early, Phyllis was awakened. "Time to get up, Robin," said Mother.

Phyllis rolled over and yawned. "Oh Mother, I'm so dreadfully sleepy, and breakfast won't be ready for a long time. Can't I sleep a little longer?" Mother pulled the covers back. "Certainly not; you are going to live like a robin now, and robins get up at four-thirty, sometimes even earlier than that, to sing. So get right up!"

Slowly, sleepily Phyllis dragged herself out of bed and wiggled into her clothes. "What shall I sing?" she asked.

"The birds always sing a hymn of praise to our heavenly Father who takes care of them. So I think some of your Sunday school songs will do," answered Mother.

All the time the robin in the apple tree

sang, Mother kept Phyllis singing. Of course, she let her rest between songs.

"Mother, I'm hungry already," said Phyllis, as she finished the last song.

"So you are," exclaimed Mother. "And as Mr. Robin is busy looking for his breakfast, you may begin to hunt yours."

Phyllis' eyes opened wide with astonishment. "Hunt mine?" she cried. "Where is it?"

"In the garden," answered Mother. "I'll show you how to find it. I have put your food in fruit jars and buried them in the ground. You must scratch until you find it. Here is my garden cultivating tool."

Phyllis took the tool soberly and began to scratch. Soon she found a jar. Opening it she ate the little bit of hard boiled egg she found inside. She felt hungrier than ever. "Mother," she called, "is this all?"

"Oh no! There's plenty in the garden, but Mr. Robin finds only a bit at a time, so you must do the same."

By eight o'clock Phyllis was tired, hot, and still hungry. She went over to the big maple tree to see if she could find some jars buried there in the shade.

"Phyllis," called Mother, "you'd better work in the sun. It's going to rain, and you'll want to get under the tree when the shower comes. A robin can't come into the house, you know."

Poor Phyllis! Hot, hungry, and tired, she just sat down and cried. She didn't hear a quick soft step beside her, but she did feel Mother's loving arms around her, and heard her voice saying, "Does my little girl want to be a robin, or Mother's cheerful little helper?"

"Oh, take me back to be your little girl! I'll dust and sweep and wipe dishes and make beds and everything if I just don't have to be a robin!" sobbed Phyllis.

Mother picked her up, big girl that she was, and carried her into the cool kitchen. She wiped her flushed face with a cool wet cloth and brushed her damp curls back where they belonged. Then she gave her a nice breakfast. Phyllis nearly went to sleep while she was eating. Mother smiled her understanding smile and led her to the sofa to take a nap.

I've never heard that Phyllis wanted to be a robin since. Of course, she gets tired of dishes sometimes, just as you do. Then Mother says softly, "Is this my little girl, or is it a robin?"

And Phyllis fairly flies at the dishes. "I'm not a robin, Mother. I won't be a robin!" she cries.

"THE ARMY CURE"

"What does this mean?" demanded Mother sternly, as she switched on the light in Joyce and Jean's bedroom.

The girls blinked and blinked their blue eyes to get adjusted to the sudden brightness. "Oh, Mother," wailed Joyce, "go down to the foot of the bed, and see if Jean isn't over on my side!"

"I'm not!" shouted Jean. "She's on my side!"

For a minute a smile played around Mother's mouth. To see both girls crowded into the middle of the bed with plenty of room on either side, was almost amusing.

Then her lips closed firmly. "This quarreling habit is going too far. Move over, both of you!" she commanded.

Sitting down by the bed she continued, "I'm going to tell you a story about the Kilkenny Cats.

"Once upon a time there were two cats. One was black with a white tip on his tail. The other was white and with a black tip on his tail.

"These cats were always fighting. When the white cat lay sleeping cosily before the fire, and the black cat came into the room, up leaped the white cat, his back humped up and his tail fluffed out, hissing, spitting, and calling the black cat all kinds of names. He acted exactly like two little girls I know."

Joyce turned her head and glanced at Jean. Jean was looking right at her. Mother went ahead as though she didn't notice.

"One day some boys saw the cats fighting in the back yard. They tied the two cats together by the ends of their tails, hung them over the wash line and left them there. 'By morning,' said one of the boys, 'they'll have had enough of fighting.'

"But when they came back in the morning to take the cats down, there was nothing left but the tips of two tails, one black and the other white. They had eaten each other up!"

"Oh, Mother!" giggled Joyce. "They couldn't have done that! Why, how could they keep on eating without mouths?"

"No," smiled Mother, "they couldn't. That's just a story. But little girls sometimes say biting things to each other, until they've nothing good left of each other. For instance, each of you said tonight that the other was selfish; and worse yet, that the other was lying. So you see that you have eaten up each other's unselfishness and truthfulness. This afternoon I heard you say, 'You mean thing!' So your kindness is eaten up too. I'm afraid some day I'll find I have no goodness left in my girls. It will all be eaten up and only badness will be left."

"Oh, how dreadful!" exclaimed Jean. "We won't quarrel any more, Mother. Really we won't."

But the very next day Jean knew it was Joyce's turn to wash the dishes. "It is not!" declared Joyce. "I washed them yesterday, so there!"

Soon angry shouts were bouncing around in the kitchen like hail on a window pane.

Mother stepped into the kitchen, her face sober and held her hands to her ears. "I thought the 'Kilkenny Kittens' had stopped fighting," she said.

Joyce and Jean paid no attention and Mother walked over to the cleaning closet. In a minute she was back with scouring powder, two small, and two large rags. "Now," she said briskly, "I'm going to try the 'Army Cure' on my 'Kilkenny Kittens.'"

Joyce's eyes grew big, and she looked at Jean anxiously. "What is Mother going to do with us?" she seemed to be saying. Jean's eyes grew big, and she gave Joyce a look that seemed to say, "What is Mother going to do, scour us?"

But no, Mother put Joyce to work on the inside of the kitchen window, and leading Jean outdoors, put her to work on the outside of the same window.

"Now girls," she said, opening the window a little, "this is what the officers in the army do when big men quarrel. You are to clean this window thoroughly. And you dare not smile at each other! You must scowl all the time. I want you to do your quarreling while the glass is between you, so you won't be able to eat each other up. What would Daddy say if he came home tonight to find nothing left of his good little girls?"

Mother took up the dish towel to do the dishes while the girls worked on the window.

Joyce and Jean found it very hard to scowl

when they had to. Jean looked so funny with the corners of her mouth turned down and her chin jutting forward. Joyce tried to hide her dimples and push her lower lip out even farther than Jean did. The faces of both little girls grew red. Their blue eyes began to twinkle and the corners of their mouths twitched. Suddenly they both burst out laughing. How foolish their quarrel seemed now!

Of course, this was just what Mother was waiting for. And since the window was sparkling by this time she called the girls in to chat with them. "You know, girls," she concluded, "you really are disobeying God when you become angry and shout nasty things at each other. In Ephesians four we are told to put such things away from us, and to be kind and tenderhearted and forgive each other. Don't you want to stop quarreling and try kindness?"

Two yellow heads nodded earnestly. "Yes, Mother, we really do want to try," said two little voices.

After that, when Joyce and Jean felt a quarrel "coming on," they would say, "We'd better not quarrel or Mother'll stop us with the Army Cure."

ONE BICYCLE
AND TWO BOYS

"Twelve dollars and fifty cents," read Donald Hillman as he picked up the tag dangling from the bicycle at Mr. Benson's secondhand store. "Isn't it a beauty, Lloyd?" he asked.

"It surely is!" agreed Lloyd. "Why that's a forty-five dollar bicycle. I'm going to take that job Mr. Jones offered me, and buy it."

"Oh, you are, are you?" exclaimed Donald. "We'll see about that. I'm going to get a job and buy it, myself. I saw it first, and it's going to be mine!"

"Easy, Sonny," mocked Lloyd. "Time enough to claim it when you get it. Before that happens, I'll earn enough money to buy it." He flung the words over his shoulder as he stamped away.

The problem of dividing one bicycle between two boys grew into a bitter quarrel between these two friends. Neither of them could afford to pay much for a bicycle, and the chance to buy a good one at that price would come only once in a lifetime.

They seldom talked or even met anymore, except by chance in front of the secondhand store. The first time this happened, Donald announced loudly, "My pay is three dollars and twenty-five cents a week. And that's more than any other merchant in town gives. He strutted around the bicycle, rubbing it here and there as though he already owned it.

"Huh! That doesn't make any difference," snapped Lloyd. "I get three dollars, and I have a dollar saved up. So you won't get ahead of me that way."

As time went on the quarrel became more bitter. The fathers of both boys talked to them seriously about spoiling a good friendship for such a selfish reason.

"Donald's wrong, Dad," declared Lloyd. "He didn't even think of buying the bike till I said I was going to get a job and buy it."

"Right or wrong, Son, a bicycle isn't worth a lost friendship. Do you realize that an honest friendship is one of the most valuable things a person can have? Besides, you know very well it's wrong to quarrel."

"I don't want his friendship, but I do want the bicycle," said Lloyd stubbornly.

Donald's father had no better success.

The baseball team suffered. Donald was pitcher and Lloyd was catcher and the two simply could not work together.

"Can't you forget that old bicycle at least until the game is over?" asked Rod Whitney, the captain of the team.

Four weeks passed. As soon as the two boys were free that Saturday night, they ran to the secondhand store, each with thirteen dollars in his pocket.

They met two blocks from the store. From

there it was a close race between them. Being equally good runners they reached the store at the same time. Mr. Benson saw them coming.

"I want to buy that bicycle!" gasped the boys in one breath.

Mr. Benson got up and tucked his shirt into his trousers before he spoke. "Sorry, boys," he answered slowly. "But the man from the city who had left it here to be sold came back this afternoon. And, of course, I had to let him have his own bicycle again."

Donald kicked at a gravel and sent it flying across the street. Lloyd pulled his bandana out of his pocket and wiped the perspiration from his flushed face. The boys looked at each other.

"Now what do you think of that?" asked Lloyd at last with a sheepish grin.

"I think a bicycle isn't worth enough to make up for losing a good friend. Especially when the bicycle belongs to someone else," Donald answered slowly.

Suddenly Lloyd's eyes lighted up as though he had a great idea. "Say, Don," he suggested, "we've got twenty-six dollars between us. Let's put it together, buy a camping outfit, and go camping at Silver Lake this summer."

"Agreed!" shouted Donald as the two old friends walked away together.

PEGGY LOU — COOK

"A really good cook, my Dear, is an artist just as truly as one who paints pictures," said Mother who was teaching Peggy Lou to make biscuit dough.

Peggy Lou looked up, her blue eyes puzzled. Then she remembered that Mother herself had painted the lovely picture in the parlor; and besides, she could make the most delicious and beautiful things to eat. "Yes," said Peggy Lou to herself. "Mother's right, and I'm going to be a good cook just like her."

"Mother," she said aloud as she folded a fat sausage into its "blanket" of biscuit dough, "I'm going to be a good cook right away. May I get breakfast all by myself in the morning?"

Mother knew that Peggy had a habit of thinking she knew all about something when she really knew very little about it. She was afraid Peggy could not get breakfast alone, so she said, "Don't you think you'll need some help? You know Daddy is very particular about his egg, and you haven't learned to cook eggs yet. You put them in boiling wa——."

"Oh, don't tell me," interrupted Peggy Lou. "Let me do it alone. You told me once that you just have to use good common sense in cooking, and I'll use my common sense to cook Daddy's egg. I can make breakfast as easy—a-as pie!"

"Very well then," agreed Mother, her blue eyes showing a sparkle of fun.

Peggy Lou had seen that sparkle before, and when Mother's eyes sparkled like that, Peggy Lou had always had trouble. But it made her all the more determined to prove she could manage breakfast by herself.

"Why," she said, as she went to bed, "it'll be easy. I know I can have Daddy's egg real soft by breakfast time. Mother'll see that I know almost everything about cooking already."

She set her alarm clock and hopped into bed. She dreamed of a land where houses were built of loaves of bread instead of bricks. The furniture was made of cookies; and soft boiled eggs, standing on end in silver holders, served as ornaments. "It's cooking land," she murmured drowsily, as her alarm went off with a musical whirr. In an instant she was wide awake. "Why did I set that alarm?" she asked, sitting up and rubbing her eyes. "Oh," she cried, jumping out of bed. "I'm getting breakfast, and I must remember about Daddy's egg."

Quickly she got into her blue-flowered dress, tied around her waist the pretty white organdy apron Mother had made, and tripped down to the spotless kitchen.

"It's kind of lonesome down here," she said with a shiver. Then she began to bustle about. Cooking cereal was no problem. She had had several lessons in that. It was soon "plopping" in the double boiler.

Making coffee was harder. She put in twice

as much coffee as Mother used, and while she was trying to keep it from boiling over, the toast burned. Just then a hissing sound made her turn to see that all the water had boiled away in the bottom of the double boiler.

"Oh, dear," she wailed. "I wish Mother would come now. But I know she won't because she never breaks her word, and she said I could get breakfast alone."

Finally after a long mixed-up time, she rang the little silver breakfast gong, half an hour late. Mother and Daddy came into the breakfast nook and sat down like company.

Daddy thanked God for the food, and Peggy Lou brought his egg. "I took special care of this, Daddy," she said, "and I know it's all right. I had a dreadful time with the rest of the breakfast, though," she added, glancing sidewise at Mother.

Mother went right ahead eating burned toast as though nothing was wrong. Peggy Lou turned back to Daddy. She had done one thing right. She knew that his egg was cooked perfectly.

Daddy gave it a quick stroke with his knife and it fell apart. The yolk was so hard that it was green on the outside!

Big tears began to roll down over Peggy's flushed cheeks onto her now limp apron. "Oh, whatever is the matter with it?" she sobbed. "I put it on to boil first thing when I came down. I was sure it would be nice and tender by breakfast. I used all my common

70

sense, and still it's boiled hard."

Mother slipped a comforting arm around the disappointed little cook. "I know you tried, Peggy Lou," she said softly. "But there are many things to learn about cooking. One of them is that the same boiling that will make one thing soft will make another hard. Eggs, as I would have told you yesterday if you had listened, must be cooked only a few minutes if they are to be soft-boiled. Daddy likes his boiled three minutes."

Peggy Lou dried her tears. "Oh, I see," she said slowly. "I'll never learn to cook," she added in discouragement.

"Oh, yes you will, if you learn one thing at a time and keep on trying," Mother assured her. "And Peggy Lou, do you know how Mother learns?"

Peggy's blue eyes opened in surprise. "Learn?" she gasped. "I thought you knew everything about cooking, Mother!"

"Cooking is a fine art, Dear, and there are always new things to learn. When I hear anyone tell of a new or different way to cook something, I listen carefully, then I try it out. So I keep learning new things all the time."

Peggy Lou sighed a big sigh. "I understand now," she said humbly. "Yesterday I wouldn't listen to you, and I knew you are a good cook. I'm going to learn, Mother, and not just know it all after this."

And Peggy Lou is a wonderful little cook today.

71

"SPECIAL DELIVERY"

"Any errands, Mother?" asked six-year-old Gordon Fisk, popping his head in at the kitchen door when he came home from school.

Mother straightened her tired back and wrung her hands out of the laundry water before she answered. "There's that basket of clothes to be delivered to Mrs. Kirby," she said. "You're so small to carry it, but I promised her she should have it before five, and this other washing has to be finished before six. I wish I could buy a wagon for you, Gordon. But since Daddy died, you know I have to save every penny. . . ."

Gordon stood up straight. "Let me try it!" he pleaded. "You said last night if we always do our best, God will help us. And I want to do it for you, Mother."

"Well," Mother answered slowly, "since there's no other way to get it there on time, you may try."

Gordon braced himself, picked up the big basket and staggered out the door with it. Mrs. Fisk's eyes filled with tears as she watched the determined little boy.

When Gordon was sure that Mother couldn't see him, he put the basket down and rested a minute. Then picking it up again, he manfully started off toward the other end of the village.

"I hope I don't meet Jud Wilkins and Sam

Brown!" he panted as he struggled along with his heavy load. "They're sure to do something, and they're so big!" Gordon shivered at the thought.

Just then around the corner came Jud and Sam!

"Ho, ho!" laughed Sam, "here's Mother's precious boy delivering the wash. Why don't you get a horse?" he mocked, seeing how hard it was for the little fellow to carry the basket.

"Here's a horse, two of 'em," cried Jud. "And here's a wagon for 'em to pull," he added dragging up their battered old wagon.

Gordon did his best to hold on to the basket, but the two boys snatched it away from him. Merrily they put it into the wagon and pranced away shouting, "We'll deliver it for him, all right, special delivery."

Gordon fought tears as he trotted along behind them. *What shall I do? How will I ever get the clothes away from the boys and deliver them at Mrs. Kirby's in time?"* he wondered.

"Say," said Sam, loud enough for Gordon to hear, "let's put this on Old Lady Crank's front porch and ring the door bell. My, won't she be mad! Ever since she broke her arm, she won't let a fellow walk within a block of her house. Won't little Gordie Fisk get a bawling out? Ho, ho, ho!" The boys doubled up laughing as they changed their course.

"Anyway, they're going in the right direction now. If they keep going this way, I might get the basket away from them and take it to

73

Mrs. Kirby on time, even yet," thought Gordon as he panted along behind the big boys.

The wagon turned a corner. Gordon followed. Then he stopped short and stood staring in amazement! There on Mrs. Kirby's porch stood the heavy basket and Sam was ringing her door bell! Quickly the two boys leaped off the porch and hid in the shrubbery to watch the fun.

Gordon dashed up the steps, wiped his hot, flushed face, and smoothed his hair back while he waited for Mrs. Kirby to open the door.

"Why, Gordon," said a surprised voice, "How did you get here so quickly? School was dismissed just twenty minutes ago. I'm so pleased to have the clothes. I just discovered that I need some of the things before five o'clock," said Mrs. Kirby as she dragged the basket into the house with her good arm.

"I-I hardly know myself, Ma'am," Gordon answered breathlessly. "I was trying to bring them, and the basket was so heavy. Then Sam and Jud came along and took it away from me and put it on your porch. They didn't know they were your clothes and thought they would make you angry. They called you Old Lady Crank, and said you'd bawl me out."

Gordon stopped short when he saw a scowl crossing Mrs. Kirby's face. "I didn't know they meant you when they said it," he added quickly.

Mrs. Kirby's brown eyes began to twinkle.

Then she laughed, invited him into the house, and gave him raisin cookies and milk. Sitting at the table while he ate, she said, "I had intended to let your mother do my washing only until my arm is well, but I have decided to let her do it all the time. And," she added, her voice trembling and a tear sliding down her cheek, "I'm going to give you Sonny's wagon so it will be easier for you to deliver clothes for your mother."

Gordon gasped. He felt like pinching himself to see if he was awake. Mrs. Kirby's only son had died just a year ago. Since then, she had shut herself up in her great house and was always sad and gloomy. She never talked to anyone about her boy or gave away anything that had belonged to him. Now she was offering him that lovely wagon every boy in the village had wanted.

Gordon gulped down the last bite of cookie and wiped his mouth with the back of his hand. "Th-thank you!" he stammered, not knowing whether to laugh or to cry.

Mother could hardly believe her eyes when Gordon came home with the fine, sturdy wagon. Her eyes filled with happy tears as Gordon told her what Mrs. Kirby had said. "God bless her," she said.

That night Gordon and Mother prayed a special prayer of thanks for the wagon which would make it so much easier for Gordon to help his mother.

"It's true, Gordon, that all things work together for good to them that love God. God always takes care of us if we do right, even when things seem to be going all wrong. Doesn't He, dear?"

"Yes, Mother," smiled Gordon as he snuggled down into his bed.

PEANUT BUTTER SANDWICHES

"Come here!" whispered Joan, beckoning to her sister Helen. And a moment later the two children, faces sparkling with mischief, peeped in at the kitchen door. Then they tiptoed into the kitchen hand in hand.

"Lucille," said Joan in a low voice, "make us two sandwiches of that please," pointing to a jar of peanut butter. "And don't tell Mother. She said we could have peanut butter only at meal time, 'cause we spoil our appetites."

"But children," began Lucille—she always called them children, to their great disgust—"you wouldn't want . . ."

"Yes we would, and hurry! Mother might come into the kitchen and catch us. Please, just this once, Lucille," coaxed Helen.

"Well," said Lucille, with a peculiar smile. "Since you insist, I'll make two sandwiches for you."

After Lucille had made the sandwiches, the girls crept cautiously to the "woods" on the lot next to the one on which their house stood. Daddy had bought the land when they were small and built a tiny playhouse there under the trees. How the girls loved their "very own woods"! There were a few big trees, many middle-sized trees, and hundreds of little baby trees. Some had only two small "leaf-hands" to lift to the sun.

"Aren't you glad we have this little house in the woods?" said Helen. "It's the best place we could find to eat our sandwiches. Say, Joan," she asked suddenly, "isn't it funny Lucille made these for us when she's always trying to make us behave? I wonder. . . ."

They set the table in the playhouse, putting on a red tablecloth and their best toy dishes. Each doll was put in her chair, and Joan in her blue dress sat down at the head of the table. Helen in her green dress took the chair at the foot.

"Now, we're ready. Bring the sandwiches, Helen, and we'll eat right away," said Joan.

The sandwiches were taken from the box where they had been hidden, unwrapped and cut into triangles. "Don't they look just too sweet on those blue plates?" exclaimed Joan.

"Patsy June," said Joan to the doll at her right, "mind your manners, Dear, and take little bites like this!" and Joan daintily nibbled her tiny sandwich.

77

"Ugh!" she cried, quite forgetting her own manners and spitting it out. "Oh, Helen, Lucille put mustard in our sandwiches! Why didn't we think? She was making deviled eggs, and of course, she was using mustard, and it looked just like peanut butter. That's why she smiled so funny."

Both the girls jumped up, gathered the remaining sandwiches and stepped outside the door. "We mustn't tell anybody about this. Jack would laugh and laugh!" said Helen as they scattered the bits of bread and mustard on the ground beneath the bushes. Joan's plump face was sober. "Do you s'pose we can get Lucille to promise not to tell on us?" she asked anxiously.

Helen laid her finger on her rosy cheek the way she did when she was thinking. "We won't go in till she calls us. Then there won't be any time to tell till after we've eaten. We can ask her right after supper," she decided.

So they sat in their playhouse for a long hour while Lucille finished preparing supper.

"Joa-an! Helen-n!" called their sister at last. The girls slipped into the house, washed their faces, and quietly sat down at their places.

Joan's blue eyes sparkled when she saw their peanut butter jar standing in front of their plates as usual. Helen's brown eyes sparkled too. They looked at each other and grinned. *That means she hasn't told,* they thought.

After Daddy had asked the blessing, the

78

girls heard a low whistle and saw Jack looking hard at the peanut butter jar.

"French's Best Prepared Mustard," he read aloud from the label turned in his direction. "Say, Sis," he asked, looking at Lucille, "what's the idea? I thought the girls didn't like mustard."

Lucille's brown eyes twinkled. "No?" she said, pretending to be surprised. "Why, they asked for mustard sandwiches this very afternoon."

"We didn't! We thought it was peanut butter! The jars are exactly alike." Then she clapped her hand over her mouth and looked at Mother. She had told on herself!

Mother asked a few swift questions and soon knew the whole story. Two guilty little girls squirmed in their chairs, wondering what their punishment would be. Mother looked at their red faces. Then turning to Lucille she said, "Helen and Joan both knew the rule about no peanut butter between meals, and they must learn to obey. Don't put any peanut butter on the table for a week, Lucille."

"We deserve it," said Helen softly when they were washing the supper dishes. And Joan nodded her head in agreement.

ONLY FIFTEEN MINUTES

"Cm'on, Dorine, it's time to get ready for the party," said Muriel.

"Yes," added Nellie. "We don't want to be late to Alice's birthday party. First thing they do is go swimming in her pool. And I just love to swim."

"I just want to finish this chapter," murmured Dorine. Turning a page she plumped her cushion, snuggled down, and was soon lost in *Little Dog Ready at Home*. When she came to the end of the chapter, she just had to know what happened when little Pep, the kitten, gave dignified old Methuselah cat's tail a quirk. So she kept right on reading.

It seemed no time at all until Muriel and Nellie were back downstairs in their crisp pink organdy dresses all ready for the party. "Dorine Baker!" exclaimed Muriel. "It's time to go right now! I'm tired of always waiting for you."

"Me too," added Nellie. "I can't remember ever going anywhere that we didn't have to wait for you!"

Dorine closed her book with a bang, bounded off the easy chair, and scurried upstairs.

Just then Mother came into the room in her pretty blue dress. "Do we have to wait for Dorine?" asked the girls in one breath. "She just now went to get ready."

After thinking a bit, Mother said, "We will

wait this time, girls, but I am going to try something, and I don't think you will have to wait for Dorine again."

"What?" cried the girls in astonishment. "What are you going to do, Mother?"

"Wait and see," answered Mother. "You two may walk home with Mrs. Jones and Becky so I can carry out my plan. Meantime we will sit here and watch the clock until she is ready."

While they are waiting, they heard slamming, thumping, and bumping as dresser drawers were jerked open and jammed shut. In her hurry to find clothes Dorine jerked a drawer all the way out. Crash! it went to the floor and clothes scattered all around. Mother, Muriel, and Nellie looked up with startled glances.

She was having a dreadful time getting ready. Grabbing her slip she dived into it only to discover she had it on backwards. "Oh, well, it won't matter," she told herself as she hurried into her crisply startched, yellow organdy dress. Glancing into the mirror she saw it did matter. The back of the slip was showing above the neckline of the dress. Quickly she jerked the buttons open, wiggled out of her dress, turned her slip around, and got into her dress again. Now the buttons didn't seem to line up. "Oh dear," she wailed, "it's inside-out." Once more the dress came off. She turned it right-side-out and put it on again. By this time its crispness was gone, and Dorine's pretty brown curls were all messed up.

Five minutes passed, and ten. More slamming and banging upstairs while Dorine searched for a second patent leather shoe which finally turned up under the bed.

Fifteen minutes had passed when at last Dorine came down the stairs. Her straggly curls dangled on the side of her head.

"You are late again, Dorine," began Mother.

"Only fifteen minutes," answered Dorine carelessly.

"But Dorine, there are three of us waiting for you. So that adds up to forty-five minutes of waiting. You have had plenty of warning, and this time you will have to take the consequences. This habit must be broken."

Dorine blinked. Was Mother going to make her stay at home and miss the party? She tried to smooth the wrinkles out of her dress, waiting to hear what the consequences would be. But Mother started off to Aunt Mae's without saying another word.

"Let's go faster," said Nellie, skipping ahead. "It's so hot, and I'm afraid we'll miss the swimming."

"Yes, thanks to Dorine!" added Muriel.

Dorine's face was red and sober as she hurried along. Changing the subject she said, "We are going to have choc'late cake and strawberry ice cream. We are going to play all afternoon, then have the party. We won't even have to help with the dishes. Won't that be nice, Mother?"

"Ye-es," Mother answered slowly. She wore such a strange look on her face that Dorine didn't know what to think.

"I thought you'd never get here," exclaimed Alice, leaving the happy group of swimmers to greet her aunt and cousins. "Come on in. The water's fine and you'll have a little time yet before the games start."

Shortly after the three girls got into the pool, Aunt Mae called everyone out to get dressed. "It's your fault we didn't get to swim longer," Muriel grumbled as she passed Dorine on her way to the house.

The afternoon passed happily. "It's four o'clock, time for refreshments now," announced Aunt Mae. Everybody skipped to the back porch where the party table was spread.

"I'm going to save lots of room for cake and ice cream," Dorine told Alice as the sandwiches were passed.

Spreading her napkin carefully she began to nibble daintily on her ham sandwich. Just then Mother leaned over and whispered, "All right, Dorine, it's time for us to leave now."

Dorine's eyes grew big and her mouth fell open. Holding her sandwich half way to her open mouth, she looked at Mother to see if she had heard right.

"That's right," Mother went on. "You see, there are only forty-five minutes of the party left and you took that much of our time before we came, so we will go now."

Dorine's face grew red. *What will everyone think if we leave now?* she wondered. Mother had already told Aunt Mae what she was planning to do, so nothing was said and no one seemed to notice when they quietly slipped outside.

Dorine's chin quivered and her eyes filled with tears when she realized Mother was missing desert too. "Couldn't *you* stay, Mother," she said in a shaky voice. "There's choc'late cake and strawberry ice cream."

"No, Dear," answered Mother. "You see, when we do wrong, it affects others too. This lesson of promptness is so important that I will be glad to miss the party if it will help you to learn it."

"Mother," said Dorine very soberly, "I will learn to be prompt. You'll help me, won't you?"

"Yes," Mother answered with her understanding smile. Then she added seriously, "But after all, it will be your own problem. One reason you are always late is that you do not keep your clothes in their proper places. Then when you are in a hurry, you can't find them. You have enough time to straighten your things while I prepare supper. There's no better time than right now to begin."

Dorine skipped upstairs and got busy. When Nellie and Muriel came home from the party, she called them into her room for a surprise. All of Dorine's clothing had been

84

picked up. Every dress hung in the closet on hangers in a neat row. Her shoes stood in a row on the floor beneath them. Every drawer held what belonged in it. Every door and drawer was properly closed.

The next time the girls were invited to a party, Dorine was the first one downstairs. Her hair was neatly combed and her dress was clean and crisp. Dorine was ready and waiting.

LOOK WHAT YOU MADE ME DO!

Gloria Jean carefully opened her birthday gift from Aunt Helen and tossed aside the pretty paper. Peeping into the box she cheered, "Oh, it's a beautiful set of pink and white doll dishes." She was bustling about setting her toy table with the new dishes when Kenneth came into the room. He walked over to look at the dishes with his hands in his pockets whistling a jolly tune.

Just then Gloria Jean dropped one of the tiny new cups. Snap! it lay shattered on the floor. "Oh, Kenneth!" cried Gloria Jean, stamping her foot. "Just look what you made me do!"

Kenneth's hands came out of his pockets. "Why, Sis," he answered, "I didn't touch your cup!"

"Yes, but you whistled, and it made me drop my cup. Mamma," she continued as Mother came to the door, "see what Kenneth made me do!"

Mother usually scolded Kenneth, knowing he was careless. But she had begun to notice that Gloria Jean always blamed someone else for her accidents. "Are you sure, Gloria Jean, it was your brother's fault?" she asked.

Gloria Jean tossed her red pigtails back. "Yes, he whistled and it made me drop my cup," she insisted.

"How could whistling made you break a cup?" broke in Kenneth.

Mother shook her head. "We'll see," she said. Turning to Gloria Jean she added, "You are to put all your toys into my work room, Gloria Jean. I'll take all my things out, and you may play there for a week. No one else will be allowed to go into the room."

Gloria Jean's brown eyes sparkled and she clapped her hands. "Goody, goody," she cheered.

"Now," Mother went on, "bring all your things to me, and I will make a list of everything you take in. At the end of the week we'll see whether anything is broken, spoiled, or lost. Then we will know whether Kenneth is to blame for your accidents."

Gloria Jean skipped about carrying her toys into the workroom. When everything had been brought and listed in Mother's notebook, she gave the little girl a key.

"Now no one but you," she said, "is to come into this room. So you may lock it while you are here, and leave it locked when you go to school."

"Won't this be fun?" Gloria Jean exclaimed to herself, as she settled down in the new room to play. "No one can bother me now, and I won't be spoiling things all the time."

She set her table again with the birthday dishes. Then she sat down with her bread and butter. "And here's a bite of cookie for each of you," she told her dolls. She reached to the far end of the table to give a bite of cookie to Aurelia, her biggest doll. When she drew her arm back, she brushed a saucer off the edge of the table. Crash! It landed on a heat pipe and shattered.

"Look what you made me do!" she exclaimed. Then her frown changed into a sheepish grin, and she burst out laughing. "There's no one but myself to blame," she told her doll family. "Do you s'pose," she said to Aurelia, "that I'm to blame all the time?"

Aurelia said nothing. She just sat up very straight in her chair and smiled her stiff smile.

Every day that week something went wrong. Gloria Jean tore Aurelia's best pink, organdy dress with the pretty roses on it. Another time she left her giant panda on the window sill. It rained that afternoon. The poor panda got soaked and left a stain on the window sill!

At the end of the week, Mother brought

her little notebook to the workroom. Gloria Jean brought each toy as Mother called its name. There were very few of her books and toys that were not damaged in some way. Some of the puzzles had pieces missing.

"Well, Gloria Jean," said Mother, showing her the list, "what do you think? Has Kenneth been causing your accidents, or are you to blame yourself?"

"I-I guess-s I am," said a small voice.

"You and I," said Mother, "will try to break this habit of blaming others. Shall we?"

"Yes," whispered Gloria Jean.

After that when Mother heard the little girl say, "Look what you made me do!" she said quietly, "What Gloria Jean?"

One night when Mother had tucked her into bed, she said softly, "Gloria Jean, do you know you are improving? You don't blame others nearly as much as you used to."

Gloria Jean's eyes sparkled and her dimples showed. "Really, Mother?" she cried. "I'm so glad. I really do try, and you always help me when I forget."

"It helps when we work together, doesn't it?" smiled Mother as she kissed Gloria Jean good night.

MARY LOU'S DREADFUL ACCIDENT

Mary Lou slung her skates over her shoulder and dashed down the back porch steps. As she ran down the sidewalk, she slipped on the ice and fell, hitting her head against her skate. Up she jumped and began to rub the bumped spot. Ooops, she found it was bleeding.

"Oh, dear," she sighed, "Mother's so particular about cuts and scratches. I'll have to go back and let her put iodine on my head. Now I'll be late to the skating party."

Mary Lou had just disappeared into the house when Estella and Geraldine came by. They saw a few drops of bright red blood on the white snow. Footprints the size of Mary Lou's led into the house. "Whatever do you suppose happened?" asked Estella.

"I don't know, but there's blood. She must have hurt herself badly," answered Geraldine.

A few blocks farther on May and Arlene caught up with them.

"Say, Mary Lou must have hurt herself. We saw blood on the snow!" exclaimed Geraldine.

"We just came down the other side of the street, and we saw a big car in front of her house. It looked like Dr. Brant's car too," said Arlene.

"She must be badly hurt then!" chimed in

Alice.

"Let's hurry to the river and tell the others," said Arlene. Away they raced and quickly told three others of Mary Lou's terrible accident. "I wonder if they'll have to take her to the hospital and have a specialist," finished May solemnly.

"Oh, how dreadful!" exclaimed Geraldine.

"Will they let us visit her and bring her flowers and fruit?" asked another.

Four newcomers were greeted with the news. "A specialist, did you say?" asked one of the older girls. "That sounds serious. She must have fractured her skull. In that case she may not live. Her poor mother. How terrible she must feel!"

"I must tell my mother," exclaimed another. She is such a good friend of the family. I know she'll want to do what she can at this dreadful time."

No one seemed to be excited about skating as they gathered in the little hut where they put on their skates. "The whole afternoon is spoiled! Let's go home. I feel like crying," said Arlene, one of Mary Lou's friends, as she began to unlace her skates.

"What are you going to cry about this lovely afternoon?" cried a cheery voice. Into the hut popped Mary Lou herself, wearing a neat gauze bandage just below her brown hair. Her dark eyes were sparkling and a bright smile lightened her rosy face.

Mary Lou was puzzled to hear all the girls

gasp. Too overcome to speak, they just stared at her. Finally someone said, "We thought you were dying in the hospital with a specialist watching over you!"

Now it was Mary Lou's turn to gasp. "Dying? Hospital? Specialist? Why, what made you think that?"

"Well, they said you had fractured your skull, and that it was serious, and, and—" the explanation trailed off into silence.

"Who said so?" demanded Mary Lou.

"I don't know—they said it," explained one of the girls in a small voice.

"I'm afraid," said sensible Emma Jane, "that we've all imagined and added until we've made a big story out of nothing. Your head is hurt, isn't it, Mary Lou? It's a wonder we had that right."

"Yes, I fell and bumped my head on my skates and cut it a little bit. You know how particular my mother is about cuts. So, of course, I had to go back into the house to have it bandaged."

"But someone said there was a big car outside your house that looked like Dr. Brant's," said Jenny.

"That was Aunt Mary's car. She came from the city to spend the weekend with Mother."

"Well, girls," said Emma Jane, "I think we should be more careful about how we tell things. Exaggeration is really lying, you know. We certainly don't want to be called liars."

"You're right, Emma," agreed Jenny. "We must be more careful after this. Let's organize a club right now. Who will be one of the 'Exact Truth-tellers'?"

The girls joined hands chanting together, "We will always tell the exact truth."

For several days Mary Lou's mother was annoyed with telephone calls. The whole village had heard about Mary Lou's accident and wanted to know how she was. Finally everyone knew that the "dreadful accident" was just an exaggerated story.

How do you suppose the girls' brothers helped them to remember their vow? For a long time they called every little mishap a "dreadful accident," and sent imaginary phone calls for a "Hospital ambulance and a specialist, quick!"

PEGGY'S ADVICE

The three little Brooks were on their way home from school. As they turned at the corner, they saw a brown car parked in front of their house. "That's Aunt Katherine's car," exclaimed Russell. "I wonder what she wants." With Russell, in the lead, Paul at his heels, and Peggy panting along behind, they raced home.

Aunt Katherine was gathering up her purse, scarf, and gloves, just ready to leave when the three children burst into the hall-way. After the hellos were said, she asked, "Would you three like to spend tomorrow with Uncle Ed, Louise, and me in the city?"

"Would we?" chorused Russell, Paul, and Peggy in one breath.

"All right," continued Aunt Katherine. "Your mother has already agreed that you may go. To add to the fun we're going to take the train and ride a trolley to the zoo like your mother and I did when we were teenagers."

"Goody, hurrah!" shouted the children.

"We will pick you up at eight o'clock sharp," Aunt Katherine went on. "Be sure to be ready. Trains won't wait and neither can we. Remember, eight o'clock sharp. Anyone who isn't ready will be left behind," she called back as she climbed into the car.

"Aunt Katherine is the nicest aunt in the whole world," announced Peggy as she watched her drive away. "Just think what fun cousin Louise and I will have spending the day together!"

"Tell you what, Peggy," said Russell. "When Mother calls you in the morning, you'd better get right up, cause Auntie said she can't wait for anyone who's late."

Peggy's brown eyes snapped, and her lower lip shoved out at Russell making him run to the sofa and hide his plump face behind a fat pillow. " 'Course I'll get up," she said indignantly.

"Peggy, oh, Peggy, time to get up, Dear!"

called Mother the next morning from the foot of the stairs. When she heard a sleepy "Yes, Mother," she hurried back to the kitchen to get breakfast on the table before little Sally awoke.

Peggy rubbed her eyes and rolled over on her side. "Ho-hum, Mother's got to get breakfast yet," she said with a big yawn. "It takes almost half an hour, and I can dress fast. So I'll just rest a little bit yet." In less than a minute Peggy was fast asleep again.

She didn't hear the boys hurrying down the stairs just as little Sally woke up and started to cry. "Go ahead and eat, boys," Mother advised. "I want to rub Sally's gums and see if I can get her to go back to sleep."

Suddenly a car horn outside awakened Peggy. She jumped and sat up in bed, trying to rub the sleep out of her eyes.

"They're here, and we're going out to the car!" called Paul from downstairs.

Peggy flew to the window and looked out to see Louise eagerly watching toward the house. Then she dived for her clothes. In her hurry she pulled two stockings over one foot and turned everything upside down looking for the other one. Her fingers seemed to be all thumbs. She got her dress on backwards. Just then Mother called, "Are you ready, Peggy?"

"I-I went back to sleep, Mother, but I'm getting ready as fast as I can," Peggy answered shakily.

"Sorry, Dear, but Aunt Katherine says they

can't wait another minute or they will miss the train," Mother answered. And she hurried back to the door to signal Aunt Katherine to go on without Peggy.

Peggy shuffled over to the window and watched the brown car speed down the street, around the corner, and out of sight. Big tears splashed down on the window sill. Laying her chubby face down among her tangled brown curls she sobbed quietly.

At last she sat back and wiggled out of her dress to put it on right. She jerked on the buttons trying to fit then into the holes. Two of them flew off and rolled away under the bed. Hot tears dashed down Peggy's cheeks and splashed on her pink dress.

"You don't need to roll like you're glad either," she muttered angrily as she watched them disappear.

After awhile Peggy slowly, slowly went downstairs. Slowly, slowly she ate her toast and drank her juice. Nothing tasted right, and it was terribly quiet with Daddy and the boys gone and Mother trying once more to rock Baby Sally to sleep.

For a long time Peggy stood with her nose flattened against the window pane. There was nothing else to do. The day seemed very long. By afternoon Sally was feeling better. She cooed and stretched her arms toward Peggy. Seeing how tired Mother looked, Peggy said, "I'll try to entertain her while your rest, Mother."

"Thank you, Dear," smiled Mother. She lay on the davenport and was soon sleeping soundly.

Peggy built block houses and let Sally throw them down. Sally squealed with delight. Peggy played peek-a-boo and patty-cake with her. The baby's face lighted up with smiles. She bounced in her swing so that her blond curls bobbed up and down. Playing with Sally was lots of fun. But when Peggy thought of the fun Russell, Paul, and Louise were having, her face grew very sober.

Taking both of Sally's little hands into her own, she looked straight into her pretty blue eyes. "Listen, Sally," she said seriously, "when you grow bigger and Mother tells you it's time to get up, don't ever think, I'll sleep a little more—not even just a teeny weeny little bit more. You might miss something really good."

Sally didn't say a word. She just pulled her little hand out of Peggy's plump one and patted her cheek to show that she agreed.

SUMMER FUN

"I wish I could go to a lake cottage this summer!" said Jim White crossly, coming in just at dinner time.

Mother looked up from the sausages she was frying, her face flushed and her eyes tired. "Why, Jim!" she asked. "What made you think of that?"

"Mark Benson's going with his uncle. And Ned and I have to stay here, same as always, working all summer."

Mother sighed. "That would be nice," she said thoughtfully. "But we don't have enough money, Jim." Suddenly her eyes grew wet and a tear darted down her face, landed on the stove, and sizzled to nothing. Quickly she turned as if to do something at the sink. But Mark knew she was trying to hide those tears. Since Daddy died her tired eyes filled with tears many times.

Just then Ned came in whistling like an oriole, his red hair rumpled like a haystack, and his eyes shining with a great idea.

"What's up now, Ned?" asked Mother, a smile spreading over her face.

"Going fishing before sunup tomorrow. May I, Mother? Come along, Jim?" he asked, scrubbing his freckled face till it shone.

"Of course," answered Mother, looking pleased.

"Sure," said Jim, staring at the floor.

Ned's haystack was smoothed down nicely now, and Jim, too, was spic and span, even if his overalls were patched and faded. Dinner was on the table. The boys folded their hands and closed their eyes while Mother thanked God for the many blessings He had sent them.

"Funny thing," said Ned over his potatoes

and sausage, "about Mark Benson. He's going to have a splendid summer at a lake cottage with his uncle. But he's just as grumpy-looking as ever, and not even excited about it. 'Course, I think I'd rather stay with you, Mumsy, if I had my choice."

Jim stopped eating and stared at his brother. "Would you really?" he exclaimed. "Why, Ned?"

" 'Cause I think it's a lot more fun," said Ned slowly, looking straight at Jim with his laughing blue eyes. "Mark's mother doesn't like for him to get dirty weeding onions or digging potatoes. But I like to get good and dirty once in a while. It feels all the better to get cleaned up again. Besides, that kind of dirt's healthy, isn't it, Mother?"

Mother nodded and Ned went on. "Poor Mark's always sick. He stays cooped up inside too much. It's the same with his uncle. They won't do anything exciting at the cottage either. Mark won't fish or row or swim all summer long. And we can do that right here, can't we, Jimmy?"

Jim squirmed in his chair. "Guess we can," he answered faintly.

"And, besides, I like to be needed," added Ned importantly, looking very much like his father. "You need us, don't you, Mother?"

"Need you, my boys?" exclaimed Mother. "I should say I do!"

Just then there was a timid knock at the door.

"Come in," called Jim. They all looked a little sheepish when Mark Benson opened the door and peeped in looking scared.

"Glad to see you, Mark," said Mother kindly. "Have dinner with us."

Mark's dark eyes sparkled. "Oh, may I?" he cried eagerly. "I'd love to."

Mother soon had a place set for him, and Ned was talking fast to make the "company" forget his bashfulness.

"That's more than I've eaten for a month," said Mark as he pushed back his plate. "Dad says things always taste better away from home. But I-I hate to bother people, Mrs. White."

"It's no trouble at all to have you," said Mrs. White. "You must come often this summer, Mark. The boys and I will be glad to have you."

"Oh!" said Mark suddenly, looking scared again. "I-I almost forgot to tell you what I came for, Mrs. White."

He stopped, his brown eyes turning to Jim then to Ned. Then he glanced toward the door as though he wanted to run away.

"What is it, Mark?" Mrs. White asked kindly.

"W-well," he stammered, his face growing red. "I-I wanted to ask you if-if I could stay here this summer, Mrs. White."

Jim's round blue eyes opened wide. "What did you say, Mark?" he gasped.

Ned ran his long fingers through his red

hair. Then he threw his head back and laughed.

Mother telegraphed to him with her eyes, "Be quiet!" and he sobered down obediently.

"You see," Mark continued, talking fast to keep up his courage, "I had a chance to go to the cottage with Uncle Mark while Mother and Dad are in Europe this summer. But it's always so poky there alone with Uncle. He never wants to do anything exciting. Besides, I like to be with other fellows. I told Mother I want to learn to swim and row and fish like Jim and Ned. And I'd like to work with the boys in the fields and get dirty this summer. So I just begged her to let me stay with you while she and Dad are away."

"And what did she say, Dear?" asked Mrs. White with her motherly smile.

"She said, 'Well go over and ask her. And tell her I'll pay her well for her trouble.' "

"Trouble?" exclaimed Mrs. White. "No trouble at all. Of course, you may come, Mark."

By this time Ned had reached the bursting point. With a wild Indian whoop he danced gaily around the table.

"Goody, goody!" exclaimed Jim. "We'll help you all we can, Mark. Whoopee, won't we have fun this summer!"

WHEN ALICE FORGOT

"I'm seven years old," said Alice, "and I've never had a doll with real hair and eyelashes, and eyes that open and shut."

Daddy looked out over his newspaper. "Why, Alice," he said in a puzzled voice, "you have such a large family of dolls already. Why should you want one more?"

"I didn't," said Alice, "till I saw that one in Morton's store window. Oh, Daddy, she's so pretty! If I could only have her for my own and wheel her around in a carriage, I'd be the happiest girl in the world!"

"What? A carriage too!" exclaimed Daddy, dropping his newspaper to look at Alice. "Too bad your father isn't a millionaire, Honey!"

A few days later Daddy brought a large parcel from the post office. "It's from your Aunt Mary in New York, and it's addressed to Miss Alice Burton," he said.

Alice's blue eyes sparkled and her dimples showed. "Help me open it quick! I can't wait to see what it is," she cried.

Mother brought the scissors to cut the cord, and the three soon had the paper off the parcel. Alice opened the top of the box and peeped in. "Oh," she gasped. "It's a doll exactly like the one in Morton's store window." Carefully pulling the doll out of the box she hugged it tightly to her breast.

Holding it out for Daddy and Mother to see she exclaimed, "Look! Real hair, eyelashes, sleeping eyes, and oh, see, her mouth is open just far enough to show her pretty white teeth and tiny tongue. It's too good to be true!"

"There's something else in the bottom of the box," Mother pointed out.

She was right. There was a small trunk full of beautiful clothes. What fun Alice had putting the different dresses and hats on her doll.

Another wonderful thing happened when Uncle Jim came to visit. Of course, Alice showed him her new doll. "She is a beauty!" exclaimed Uncle Jim, stroking the brown curls. "What are you going to call her?"

"*Alicia*, after me. I'm her mother, you know," she answered proudly.

"Of course," agreed Uncle Jim, his hazel eyes twinkling. "You must have a doll carriage for her, so you can take her out to get fresh air."

"Oh!" exclaimed Alice, catching her breath.

The very next day Uncle Jim came home with the nicest carriage he could find in the village. It was a pretty wicker one, with a glass window on each side of the hood and a curtain at the back to shut out the light and the cold air. Alice could peep in at the window to be sure that Alicia was cozy and comfortable.

But for a long time Alice had had a problem remembering to put her things away when she was finished playing. She would leave her toys right where she had been playing.

"Alice will be more careful now," Mother

told Daddy. "Surely she will remember to put things away since she has that wonderful doll and carriage."

For a whole week Alice put her things away every single time without even being told. But one evening she forgot. She went to bed and left her doll and carriage outside on the porch.

When Daddy came home late that night, Alice had been asleep for hours. He usually came in at the side door when he was late. Tonight he did not stop to turn on the porch light. Smack! He walked right into the doll carriage. It tipped over on its side. Crash! Daddy came down on top of it. It was badly smashed, and one of the windows was broken.

Mother, hearing the noise, ran toward the porch turning on lights as she went. There she found Daddy, doll, and carriage all on a heap.

"Are you hurt?" cried Mother anxiously.

"I don't think so. Not much," said Daddy, picking himself up. "But what will Alice say?"

Mother started to pick up the broken pieces, then changed her mind.

Alice awoke early and got into her yellow dress. Alicia had one almost like it, and they would be dressed alike today.

"Mother-r!" she called a few minutes later. "I can't find Alicia or the carriage anywhere. Do you know . . .?"

She stopped short at the look on Mother's face. "Why, Mother," she cried, "did something happen to Alicia last night?"

"I'm very sorry, Alice," she began gently. "You left them on the porch last night, right in the path to the side door. When Daddy came in late, he fell over the carriage. He could have been hurt. I'm glad it's not Daddy that is broken!"

Together they went out to the porch and looked at the smashed carriage and the broken doll.

Alice burst into tears, dashed to the sofa, and hid her face in a pillow. Mother felt badly too, but she said nothing.

Alice sobbed for a long, long time. At last she sat up, blew her nose, and wiped her tears. Then tossing back her golden curls she got a box and went back to the porch. Slowly, slowly she picked up the broken bits of poor Alicia and the pieces broken off the carriage.

Putting them together in a box she said sorrowfully, "I know it's my fault. But I did love them so! I guess I'll keep the pieces a while—to help me remember to put my things away."

"BAREFOOT BOY"

"Mother," teased Louis one night, "Mickey and Peter both came to school barefoot today. Couldn't I try it just once?"

"Not yet, Louis," Mother answered. "You

see, Mickey and Peter are stronger than you, and it doesn't hurt them. But remember the croup you had last winter?"

Louis said nothing aloud, but he was thinking. "I'll do it just once and show Mother it won't hurt me."

The next noon instead of going out the front door and down the street to school, Louis slipped through the back yard. Glancing back toward the house to be sure Mother wasn't looking, he dived into the old chicken house.

"This is the best place I could ever find," he said aloud. "Nobody comes in here since the chickens were sold. I'll put my shoes and stockings into this old nest and cover them with straw. Nobody will ever find them."

After hiding his shoes, Louis opened the door and peeped toward the house once more. No one was in sight, so he quickly climbed the back fence and went down the alley.

"Ow! these cinders are sharp. I almost wish I had my shoes on again. But it's too late to go back after them now," he thought.

He stopped at Mickey's house down by the river to wait for him. "Why, Louis!" exclaimed a surprised voice, and he turned to see Mickey's big sister coming out at the side door. "Does your mother know you are barefoot so early in the spring?" she demanded. He felt as though her dark eyes were looking right through him.

"Mickey was yesterday," answered Louis.

"Yes, but that's different. Mickey is used to it. He never catches cold as you do. You mustn't try to do as Mickey does. He's a tough little fellow." And she smiled fondly at her sturdy little brother who came out just then.

"Louis," asked Mickey a little later, "did your mother really let you go barefoot?"

"No, I had to sneak away," stammered Louis. "My mother never lets me go barefoot until June. But I'm not a baby. I won't catch cold."

"Don't mind what my sis says. She always thinks a fellow's doing wrong. Surely it's all right to do what you want to with your own feet," said Mickey comfortingly.

Louis wondered what the boys would think when they saw him barefoot like Peter and Mickey. He was disappointed when nobody seemed to notice.

Seated at his desk in the schoolroom, Louis began to feel very uncomfortable. He glanced up at Miss Burke. She was watching him. It seemed to him that she had a queer look on her face. When he was called on to recite, all the girls seemed to look at his feet. Once he even thought he heard his name and a little titter of laughter after it.

Poor Louis! He felt as though his feet were getting bigger and bigger. "Can I ever squeeze them into my shoes again?" he wondered.

School was dismissed at last. Louis went home through the alley, cut across a neighbor's yard, and climbed over the fence. Glancing toward the kitchen window he sneaked into the chicken house.

"Whee! am I ever glad I didn't get caught!" he sighed. "Going barefoot isn't as much fun as I thought it would be. I'll get my shoes and stockings on quick before Mother sees me. Wh-what!" he exclaimed, as he felt around in the nest where he had hidden the shoes. They were gone!

Quickly he pulled the straw out of every nest in the old chicken house. "Oh, dear," he said aloud. "Somebody's stolen them. I wonder if that Tad Bloom. . . ."

"Louis, oh, Louis!" called Mother's voice from the house.

No reply.

"Louis!" her voice was stern and sharp now, and he dared not wait any longer to answer.

"Yes," he said faintly.

"Come into the house instantly."

"I-I can't," he said, his voice shaking. And once again he searched frantically through the nests.

"Why can't you?"

"Because. . . ."

"What are you doing in the chicken house?"

"I-I'm just looking for something."

"Louis," said Mother, "if you are looking for your shoes, you will find them right here in the house."

He was caught!

But how did she find out? he wondered as he walked slowly, slowly toward the house.

Mother's usually happy face was very sober as Louis sat down and with shaking fingers tried to get into his socks and shoes. His thin face was red and the corners of his eyes were wet. The kitchen was so quiet that the slow ticking of the clock could be heard. Mother just stood there watching without saying a word.

At last she said, "I'm very sorry to find that you can't be trusted, Louis." Then by her questions he knew she knew exactly what he had done.

"But who told you, Mother?" he asked tearfully.

"I'm afraid you care more about being caught than you do about having misbehaved," Mother answered slowly. "But, really, you can be thankful that you were caught the first time you tried to deceive me, Son. Mrs. Wells informed me soon after lunch that she saw you coming out of the chicken house in your bare feet. So I went out and found your shoes and socks just where you had left them.

Louis kept right on struggling with his shoes, his face down so Mother couldn't see how red it was. It seemed as though his fingers were all thumbs.

"You know," Mother continued, "the Bible says, 'Be sure your sin will find you out.' And yours surely has. I hope you will always remember that verse and the lesson you have learned."

At last Louis' shoes were tied. Tears were spilling from his eyes as he looked up into Mother's still sober face.

"I will, Mother!" he stammered. "It wasn't even any fun going barefoot. The fellows didn't even notice, and the girls made fun of me. I'm sorry I disobeyed and deceived you, Mother. And I promise I won't go barefoot again till you say that I may!"

"JUST ONCE"

"I'm not going to school tomorrow," announced Marilyn as she came in one Thursday afternoon. She threw her books onto the dining room table as if to show that she meant just what she said.

"Is it some kind of holiday?" asked Mother.

Marilyn toyed with the ribbon on the front of her dress. "No," she answered.

"Are the teachers having a convention or something?" Mother asked.

Marilyn tossed back her hair and shook her head, "No. I'm just not going."

Mother's brown eyes shone with interest and questions. "I don't understand. You never wanted to miss school before. Do you intend to stay at home without any excuse?"

Marilyn plopped down into the nearest chair. "Well, none of the other girls are going," she announced.

"None of them?" Mother's voice sounded doubtful.

"The girls I go with," Marilyn hurried to explain.

"Why not?" Mother questioned.

Marilyn smoothed the pleats in her blue dress. "We just don't want to go, Mother. I never skipped school in my life and I want to see what it's like. I don't want always to be a goody-goody."

Mother could hardly believe her ears. But Marilyn went on, "Another thing, all the girls are planning to make candy at Joan's house. Her mother works, and Donna and Loey say their mother won't be home, so there'll be nobody to ask questions. Carol's mother went to the country and Judy's mother is in the hospital. We might even send some candy to her."

"But, Marilyn, what shall I say when Miss Gray calls from school to ask why you are absent? You know they always check up on absentees," Mother added.

"Oh, just tell her anything. The other girls are trying to think up some good excuses and plan to answer the phones themselves."

"Marilyn!" exclaimed Mother in a shocked voice. "I never could do that. Surely you wouldn't want me to tell a lie. I'll just say you're at Joan's house making candy."

Marilyn's blue eyes snapped. "But, Mother, you don't understand. I want to see what it's like to skip school. Judy says every girl should have a chance to do it at least once in her life." With a quick grab she snatched her books and ran upstairs to her room. No more was said the rest of the evening about missing school.

The next morning Mother called Marilyn as usual.

"But, Mother, don't you remember? I'm not going to school today. Please, please let me go to Joan's house!"

"Come, Marilyn. Daddy likes for you to eat breakfast with us. Don't disappoint him," Mother answered.

A big frown crowded all of Marilyn's dimples from her face. Then an idea popped into her mind. "I'll get ready just as usual," she told herself. "Then after Daddy leaves I'll persuade Mother to let me skip school."

The sparkling orange juice and beautifully browned toast on the table in the sunny kitchen looked very inviting. Daddy's pleasant smile and cheery "good morning" gave

111

Marilyn such a warm feeling that she was glad she had gotten up for breakfast.

Right after breakfast Daddy reached for the Bible as he always did. "Children, obey your parents in the Lord: for this is right," he read. Marilyn looked hard at the checkered red tablecloth and squirmed in her chair. Why did he have to read that this morning?

Right after Daddy left, Marilyn hurried to her room. Soon Mother called, "Marilyn, your lunch is ready. Come, you don't want to be late."

Marilyn got her sweater and slowly picked up her books. Walking over to Mother she begged, "Why do I have to go, Mother?" Tears spilled from her eyes as she continued, "I'd love to know how it feels to skip school just once."

Mother's kind eyes looked right into Marilyn's teary ones. "Because it's the right thing to do. And I think you will be glad you did, Dear," she answered, handing her her lunch.

"It was just as I expected," exclaimed Marilyn when she came home that Friday afternoon. "None of the girls were in school, and they didn't get caught either!"

The next Friday Marilyn was ill. As the day wore on, she began to feel better. "I wonder if the girls skipped school again," she said. "It was so easy last week. They were planning to try it again."

Just then the telephone rang. Marilyn knew it was Miss Gray calling, because she heard Mother say, "Marilyn is ill; she has not been able to be up all day."

On Monday afternoon Marilyn danced in from school excitedly. "Guess what, Mother! Miss Gray told me that our home was the only one she called on Friday. She said she went in person to see all the other absentees. The girls decided it isn't so much fun to skip school after all."

"I'm sorry for them," remarked Mother, "not that they were caught, but because they did wrong."

"Yes," said Marilyn thoughtfully. "Miss Gray says it will mean a week of detention for every one of them. Just think of that, Mother. Studying after school every day for a whole week—and it's spring!"

"I'm getting happier all the time that you didn't stay home that day, Dear!" said Mother with her friendly smile.

Marilyn's blue eyes were thoughtful. "Yes, Mother, so am I. But what makes me happiest of all is that Miss Gray just telephoned instead of coming to see me. It feels so good to be trusted."

HOW A TALE GROWS

Jean usually walked home from school with her brother John. But today she was alone.

"Where's John?" asked her friend Mary, joining her.

"Oh, his teacher asked him to stay after school. I hope he wasn't a bad boy," Jean answered as she turned in at her own yard.

"I wonder," said Mary going on alone. She picked up speed and caught up with Arthur. "John was kept after school for being bad," she told him.

Arthur stopped whistling a merry tune and stared at Mary. "That's hard to believe!" he exclaimed. "What did he do?"

Mary blinked her big brown eyes. "I don't know. But when I was going back to school after lunch, I saw a broken window in Mr. Smith's house. I wonder if John broke it."

Arthur hurried on to the vacant lot where the boys were playing ball. "Hello, Arthur!" called Jim. "Where's John?"

Arthur waited to answer until he was closer. "John broke Mr. Smith's window, and the teacher kept him after school," he announced in a shocked voice.

"You don't say!" cried Jim. "That doesn't seem like him."

Jim ran over to Joe. "John broke a window," he said. "That means he stole five dollars."

"How do you know?"

"Mr. Smith told my mother someone broke his window and took five dollars from the table beside it. His wife was in town and he was in the field when it happened."

"I'd never believe it of John," said Joe thoughtfully, "if I hadn't heard it with my own ears. I wonder what else he did."

"I've no idea. But I think Mr. Smith ought to know John broke that window. Otherwise, he might think we did it," said Jim.

"That's right. Let's go over and tell him as soon as this game's over," added Arthur.

Arthur and Jim and Joe ran over to Mr. Smith's house talking excitedly all the way. "I really hate to tell on John," said Arthur. "He's always been nice to me."

"Me too," added Jim. "But I think Mr. Smith really should know."

"That's right," Joe agreed. "Besides, if John gets caught this time he won't be trying something else soon!"

Mr. Smith was surprised to see three excited boys bounding up his steps and onto the porch. He invited them into the house and listened quietly to their story. His face became more and more sober as the story came out.

"Can you boys prove what you have just told me?" he asked.

The three boys looked from one to another. All they knew was that John was kept after school, that a window had been broken, and the money had been taken. Wasn't that enough?

Mr. Smith cleared his throat and rubbed his strong farmer hands together. "Sit down, boys," he said. "I want to talk to you. Someone started a tale. It grew and grew, and John is made out to be a thief. Do you think that's fair?"

The three boys looked at each other's red faces. "But you told my mother," began Jim, "that someone came and broke your window and took five dollars—"

"I said I found a window broken and the money gone. I accused no one, though as you can see, it did look very much like a theft," answered Mr. Smith.

"If John didn't take the money, then do you know who did?" asked Arthur.

"Yesterday I ordered chicken feed, and I knew the man would deliver it today. I left five dollars on the table by the window and asked my wife to pay him when he came. She was just ready to leave for town when he brought the feed."

" 'Put it in the barn,' " she said as she ran to get the money. In her haste she knocked over a vase. It fell against the window and broke it.

"When I came in from the field, I found the window broken and the money gone. That's all I knew. Just then your mother came in, Jim. She brought some sugar to pay back some she had borrowed. I told her about the broken window and the money.

"A few minutes later my wife came home.

She said the feed had come and explained how the window was broken."

They all looked out the window as they heard someone come by whistling. It was John!

"Shall we call him in and talk it over?" asked Mr. Smith.

Three red-faced boys nodded in agreement. John stopped whistling when he heard his name called. "Can you stop a minute, Son?" asked Mr. Smith.

"Of course, but I can't stay," John replied cheerfully. His blue eyes grew round with surprise as he looked from Arthur to Jim, from Jim to Joe. Why were they here, and why did they look as though they wished they were somewhere else?

"Son," Mr. Smith began, "you were kept after school today, weren't you? I've no idea why. Would you mind telling these boys the reason?"

"Oh, that! Why, my teacher just wanted me to help carry home some plants she ordered at the store this morning. And she gave me a great big piece of cherry pie. That was good pay; don't you think so, Mr. Smith?"

BE KIND

"Come on, Ray!" Reid shouted to his brother. "The boys are playing ball. Get your glove and let's go."

"Uncle Byron is weeding his beets," replied Ray. "I think I'd better go and help him; he said yesterday his back ached."

"Don't be silly, Ray Parker!" exclaimed Reid, rumpling his red hair. "Catch me missing a ball game to help an old man weed his beets!" With that he picked up his ball and was off.

"Where's Ray?" chorused the boys when Reid came in sight. "We need him to be catcher."

"I told him to come, but he's gone to help Uncle Byron. Why he wants to bother with that old man, I'm sure I don't know. I wouldn't," exclaimed Reid.

"Is he really your uncle, Reid?" asked Jimmy Platter.

"No. He's been our next door neighbor ever since I can remember. We boys have always called him uncle."

"Do you like him?" Tommy Sebold wanted to know.

"Sure, but not enough to help him weed his old beets when I can play ball. He doesn't have much to do. Let him pull his own weeds," Reid replied.

Some of Mr. Byron's neighbors said he was stingy and never spent any money on himself.

Others thought he was not friendly because he was shy and did not talk a lot. The truth was that he was often lonely.

Mrs. Parker always treated her neighbor kindly. She often sent over something good for him to eat. She wished she could do more for him, but she was very busy working to support her sons.

"Why, Ray!" cried Uncle Byron joyfully as Ray dropped down beside him in the beet row and began to pull weeds. "I didn't expect to see you this morning. Aren't the boys playing ball at the corner?"

"Yes, Uncle Byron," said Ray.

"Reid's playing with them, I suppose?"

"Yes. Reid would hate to miss a ball game."

"Guess he's not the only one that doesn't like to miss ball games," the old man spoke half to himself.

"What was that you were saying, Uncle Byron?" asked Ray.

"Oh, nothing much. Kind of a habit of mine, Ray, thinking out loud."

One row of beets was nearly finished when Ray heard someone calling frantically. "Help! help! Ray! Ray! Come quick!"

"Uncle Byron," Ray exclaimed, "I think someone must be hurt. I'll run and see what's the matter."

Before Ray reached the corner lot where the boys were playing ball, he bumped into Ted. "Reid's hurt," he exclaimed, panting. "We-we think his leg's broken. What shall we do?"

Ray's eyes grew wide with fright and his cheeks turned pale. "Mother's at work," he gasped. Then in a relieved voice he added, "I'll tell Uncle Byron. He'll know."

It took only a minute to run back and tell Uncle Byron. He dropped his hoe and began to give orders. "Run over and tell Mrs. Price to call the ambulance, then get some towels and a blanket of your mother's and come to the corner as quickly as you can!" With that he picked up a piece of board and hobbled toward the corner as fast as he could with his aching back and stiff legs.

Ray followed Uncle Byron's instructions and reached the corner at the same time the old man did. With Uncle Byron directing and helping they cushioned the board with towels and tied the broken leg securely to the board. "I-it feels some better now," sobbed Reid trying to fight back the tears. Uncle Byron put the blanket on him and tried to soothe him until the ambulance arrived.

"That was a fine job of first aid. You saved the lad a lot of suffering by putting on that splint," said the ambulance driver.

Reid was soon in the hospital. "It's a very bad fracture. He will have to be in bed a long time to allow the bone to knit properly," explained Dr. Jarvis.

One afternoon when Ray and Mother were visiting Reid at the hospital, Mother said, "I don't know what I'd do if it weren't for Uncle

Byron. He already paid the doctor, and he wants to take care of the hospital bill too. They say a friend in need is a friend indeed. He certainly has proved to be one to us. I'd have managed to get along some way, but he surely has taken a heavy load off my shoulders."

Reid turned his pale face away.

"What is it, Reid?" asked Mother. "Does your leg hurt much?"

Reid rubbed the tears out of his eyes with his fists. "No, Mother, it's not my leg. But I've been such a mean boy. I've been thinking about it ever since I'm in here."

"You haven't been unkind to Ray, have you?"

"No, but I was unkind to Uncle Byron. I called him a stingy man, and I never did anything to help him."

"He surely is good to you, isn't he?" remarked Ray.

"I should say he is!" sobbed Reid. "He comes to see me every day. He brings fruits and games and books. And now he's paying for everything!"

"I'm sorry you've talked about him," said Mother. "But I'm sure you'll never do such a thing again. Uncle Byron has taught you a lesson you will always remember."

"Uncle Byron knows a lot, Mother," said Ray. "That day I helped him weed his beets, he told me things I never knew before. And he knew exactly what to do when Reid was hurt!"

"Yes, Son. Old people have learned many things during their long lives. And it's wise to listen to all they have to tell us. But even more important than that, we should always be kind to them."

"Ray was kind to Uncle Byron," said Reid, "and now Uncle Byron is kind to me. I hope I can do something for him soon. Are his beets all weeded yet?"

Mother smiled. "He won't need your help in his garden, Reid, at least until your leg is quite well. But there will be plenty of things to do for him as well as for other elderly people."

"Every time I see Uncle Byron, she added, "I think of some lines that my teacher wrote on the blackboard one day when I was a little girl.

"Be kind and be gentle to those who are old,

For kindness is dearer and better than gold."

"We will, Mother, we will!" promised Reid and Ray in one breath.

AN ARROW GOES ASTRAY

Frank's brown eyes sparkled as he rubbed and rubbed the smooth bow Uncle Bob had brought for his birthday. He picked up the arrows and turned them from side to side admiring their feathers. "What are the feathers for, Daddy?" he asked.

"Feathers keep the arrow straight on its course as it sails through the air," Daddy explained. "That is why it is important never, never to use anything but an arrow with your bow. Two things you should always remember: be sure there is no one nearby who may be hurt by your arrow, and never use a stick or other object which might go off to a side and hit someone.

One day several weeks later Mother announced, "I'll have to go to town this afternoon. There isn't time to take you along, but I won't be gone long."

"That's all right, Mother. We'll be all right," answered Frank and Carol. They waved as Mother drove down the lane.

For some time the children kept right on playing house in the old trailer. Old zinc jar lids were just the right size for chocolate mud pies. Fennel blossoms made nice fried eggs, and daisies turned out to be dainty layer cakes.

Frank made a set of little cups by cutting off one end of smooth brown acorns and hollowing them out. The flattened acorn caps made pretty little saucers.

"Oh, what a lovely tea set!" exclaimed Carol, her dimples showing.

"Now I'll take my bow and arrow and hunt a wild turkey like the Pilgrims did to go with the dinner you are cooking," said Frank.

Carol tossed back her blond pigtails. "Please do," she replied. "I've been hungry for wild turkey for a long time."

Frank got his bow and arrow and began stalking a sparrow that was hopping about.

Carol's blue eyes clouded with pity, "Please don't hurt the sparrow!" she exclaimed.

No answer. The sparrow flew up to a shrub and Frank aimed. His aim was too high, and the arrow landed on the chicken house roof. "My only arrow gone and I missed my turkey!" he cried.

Carol picked up a nice straight stick. "Use this for an arrow," she suggested. "But please shoot a turkey instead of a sparrow!"

Frank ran his hand back and forth on the bow. He looked at the stick and remembered Daddy's warning, "Never use a stick for an arrow."

Ordinarily Frank obeyed his father. But this time he was in a hurry, and Carol must have that turkey for dinner! *What will it matter if I use a stick just this once?* he reasoned. Taking the stick he began to stalk the sparrow again.

Carol was setting the table and needed some big plantain leaves for plates. She ran to get some that grew behind the barn.

She darted out from behind the barn, her hands full of leaves just as Frank fired his stick-arrow. Like a flash the stick sped through the air turning aside toward the barn.

124

The sparrow flew away. But poor Carol! The leaves scattered and she screamed, "Oh! Oh! My eye! My eye!"

Frank was horrified. Dropping his bow he raced toward the screaming little girl.

Just then Mother drove in. She saw at once that something serious had happened. Moments later she and the children were in the car speeding to the hospital. Carol was in great pain, but poor Frank felt worse than she did.

He knew without being told that Carol might lose the sight in her injured eye. How could he bear it if she did?

Mother, noticing the white-faced boy by the window, moved closer to him and laid her arm across his shoulder. Together they bowed their heads in prayer for the little girl that had been wheeled through the long hall and disappeared behind closed doors.

Through tears Frank watched the clouds hurrying past the window. Every time a white-clad nurse passed, he turned eagerly, hoping she would bring good news about his little sister.

It seemed hours before the kind old doctor came out to the waiting room. His eyes looked tired. "Your daughter will be all right, Mrs. Kelly," he said. "That was a close call, though."

Frank buried his face in his hands and sobbed with relief. Carol would not be blind! Oh, it was too good to be true! Finally he lifted his head and looked at Mother. She smiled and he smiled back. Her arm tightened around his shoulder as she drew him close.

Then bowing their heads, closing their eyes, and sitting hand in hand, they prayed. A nurse in white tiptoed by reverently. "Dear God," Frank prayed, "thank You for saving Carol's eye. Please forgive me for disobeying Daddy and hurting her. And please help me always to obey Daddy. In Jesus' name. Amen."

"I LOVE YOU, MOTHER!"

"Tomorrow's the day!" shouted Eunice, hopping about on one foot. "I thought it would never come!"

"What day?" asked Mother as she lifted little Tommy out of his high chair.

"Mother's Day, of course! We can say our pieces without a mistake, can't we, Janice? You'll just love our twin recitation, Mother. It's all about you, every word!"

Mother looked at the breakfast table which was waiting to be cleared. Soon she would have to give Tommy his bath. And there were so many other things to do! "I'm sorry, Dear, but I'm afraid I won't be able to go to the program."

"Why, Mother?" asked Janice in surprise.

"Well, Tommy kept me awake a long time

last night. If I should go, I'd have to get most of Sunday's dinner ready today. I'm almost too tired to do that with all the other work I have to do."

"Now, Mother," cried Russell, "what do you think we're having a program for anyway? It's specially for Mothers. You'll just have to go."

Mother held her hand to her head and sighed, "Well," she replied slowly, "it will depend on you, all three of you. If you help me enough today, I may be able to manage."

Three sets of brown eyes sparkled eagerly. "We'll help you all right, Mother," they promised.

"The first thing then, is to get the table cleared and the dishes washed," Mother directed.

Suddenly Eunice laid her finger on her cheek the way she did when she thought of something. "Oh, Jan!" she exclaimed. "You clear the table while I run down to Evelyn's for a minute. I have to take care of something!"

"But, Eunice, dear," began Mother.

"I'll be right back, Mother. I have to see about the carnations for the drill." Tossing back her brown curls and snatching her sweater she was gone.

Janice's brown eyes clouded. "Did you ever see anybody run away so fast?" she exclaimed. Reaching for a barrette to keep back her brown curls, she added, "I'm sorry,

Mother. I know she won't hurry back. But I'll help you as much as I can."

"I know you will, Dear," smiled Mother. "I can always depend on you when there's work to be done."

Mother turned to tell Russell what he could do to help, but he, too, had disappeared.

Janice put on her yellow apron and went to work at once. But little hands cannot work as fast as large ones. It was late when the last dish was put away and the kitchen was in order.

Tommy was cross all morning. Mother had to leave her work many times to quiet him, so she wasn't able to get very much done.

While Janice was setting the table for lunch, the door flew open and in rushed Eunice, all out of breath. "I didn't mean to stay so long, really! We were talking about tomorrow, and practicing the drill, and, oh, everything! The first thing I knew, Evelyn's mother called her to come to lunch."

Just then Russell bounced in, his brown hair standing up like a haystack, all out of breath. "I had to run down to Jim's and get my bag of marbles; I left it there last night."

"But, son," began Mother.

"I meant to help you, Mother. Honest! But we played just one game, then one more. Somehow we kept on playing. I was really surprised when Jim's sister called him to lunch."

Mother smiled a tired smile and sighed.

"You make me think of a poem that was in my reader when I was a little girl." Slowly she began to recite.

"I love you Mother," said little John;
Then, work forgotten, his cap went on,
And he was off to the garden swing,
Leaving his mother the wood to bring.

"I love you, Mother," said little Nell;
"I love you better than tongue can tell."
Then she teased and pouted half the day,
Till Mother was glad when she went to play.

"I love you, Mother," said little Fan;
"Today I'll help you all I can."
Then to the cradle she quietly crept
And rocked till the baby sweetly slept.

Next, stepping softly, she took the broom
And swept the floor and dusted the room.
Busy and happy all day was she,
Helpful and cheerful as child could be.

"I love you, Mother," again they said,
Three little children going to bed.
How do you think that Mother guessed
Which of them really loved her best?

No one said anything for a moment after Mother finished the poem.

Eunice's face was sober. "Mother," she said slowly, "you don't really think Janice is the only one in this family that loves you, do you?"

"What do you think about it, Dear?" asked Mother.

"Well, I guess it looks that way. But we still

have the afternoon, and I mean to show that I love you," declared Eunice.

"Me too," agreed Russell.

After lunch Eunice put her brown curls into a barrette and got into an apron. "I want to do these dishes alone to make up for running away this morning," she explained.

Russell took the grocery list to the store and brought the groceries home in his red wagon. "Do you think I can put these things away all right, Mother?" he asked.

"Certainly, you can," she replied. "If you don't know where something belongs, just ask."

Janice rocked Tommy until he went to sleep. Mother vacuumed the floors and Eunice dusted all the furniture.

When Daddy came home, the house was shining. Everyone wanted to tell him how it had all come about. "I did wrong, Daddy, when I ran off all morning instead of helping Mother," Eunice confessed.

"And I did wrong too," echoed Russell. "I'm really sorry."

"They're forgiven now, aren't they, Mother?" asked Daddy.

"Yes, indeed!" smiled Mother. "They have all showed they really do love me. It's the best gift I've ever had in my life."

"I want a share in this helping business," declared Daddy. "Tomorrow really will be Mother's Day at our house. I'll take care of Tommy and get dinner."

"Da-da!" gurgled Tommy.

"Then Mother can go to the program!" shouted Russell.

"She certainly can," Daddy agreed. "And when it's over, she'll come home and have a good rest."

"We'll wash all the dishes, won't we, Janice?" squealed Eunice, grabbing her twin around the waist and almost hugging the breath out of her.

"No," said Russell. "You and I, Eunice. Janice earned a vacation, along with Mother."

Mother's eyes sparkled and she smiled a big, big smile. It wasn't a tired smile this time. "No one in all the world ever had a finer family," she exclaimed happily.

BIBLE STORIES
for
CHILDREN

A BEAUTIFUL GARDEN

A long, long time ago God made a beautiful garden in the land of Eden. All kinds of trees that were good for food and trees that had pretty flowers were planted there. God placed two special trees in the middle of the garden. One was called the Tree of Life and the other the Tree of Knowledge of Good and Evil.

How beautiful the garden was! Every kind of delicious fruit hung from the branches of the trees. A beautiful river flowing through the garden separated into four smaller rivers. The dainty blossoms growing along the riverside reflected in the shining waters. Brilliant fish darted about over the rocky bottom, and large trees shaded lovely pools where water lilies grew. Everything was fresh and new. No withered flowers or grass marred the beauty.

The Lord gave the garden to Adam, the man He had made, and told him to take care of it. He showed him the fruit trees. Then God took Adam to one tree in the middle of the garden. He gave Adam permission to eat the fruit of all the trees in the garden except this one. "If you eat the fruit on this tree," God said, "in that day you will surely die." Adam was very careful not to touch that fruit.

The Lord felt sorry for Adam when He saw him alone in the garden. He brought all the animals to him so he would name them.

Among all the animals there was not one that was suitable to help Adam and be a friend to him. So God put him to sleep, took out one of his ribs, and made another person. When He showed her to Adam, He said, "She shall be called woman, because she was taken out of man." Later, Adam named her Eve. They lived together very happily in the garden. No weeds grew there, and it was easy to take care of.

One day when Eve was walking alone among the trees, she met a snake. Was she afraid? No. Nothing had ever hurt or frightened her. The snake was very crafty and began to talk to her. He asked whether God had said they were not allowed to eat of every tree in the garden.

"Yes, we may eat the fruit of all except one," Eve answered. "God says if we eat of it or even touch it we shall die."

Then the snake looked very wise and said. "That isn't true. You will not die. I know what will happen. God knows that when you eat that fruit you will be much wiser than you are now. In fact, you will be as wise as God Himself, and you will know right from wrong."

Then Eve made a big mistake. She turned to look at that tree. The fruit did look good to eat, and the snake had said it would make her wise. Slowly she reached out her hand and touched the fruit. Then she took hold of it and plucked it off. It really did look good as she slowly turned it in her hand. She took a bite. She took some to Adam and he ate it too.

And then what do you suppose happened? Adam and Eve were miserable. They knew they had done wrong. They were afraid of God. They could not enjoy walking and talking with Him in the garden as they had before. So they hid themselves. When God came into the garden in the evening to talk with Adam, He could not find him. God called, "Where are you?"

Adam answered, "I heard You coming and I was afraid, so I hid."

God knew Adam would not be afraid of Him unless he had disobeyed. "Did you eat of the fruit I told you not to touch?" He asked.

Adam was just like many people today. He did not like to admit he had done wrong. So he said, "The woman You gave me took some of the fruit and gave it to me, and I ate it."

Then God asked Eve, "What is this that you have done?" Eve, like her husband, blamed someone else. "The snake told me it was good, so I ate it," she said.

God was very angry with all three of them. He told the snake that he must crawl on the ground and eat dust for his food. He also said that the woman and the snake should always hate one another.

He told Adam and Eve they must leave the beautiful garden and go out into the world to make a living for themselves. Thorns, briers, and thistles would come up in Adam's fields.

He would have to work hard in the hot sun to raise his crops so they would have something to eat. Not only would Eve have to leave her happy home in the garden, but she would have sorrow and trouble all her life.

When they had gone out of the garden, God put an angel at the entrance with a fiery sword in his hand so Adam and Eve could never come back again

SHEPHERDS OF BETHLEHEM

It was night. Except for the occasional bleating of a lamb everything on the hillside was quiet.

Suddenly a great white light flooded the hillside. Startled, the shepherds jumped up, grabbed their staffs and stood staring with frightened eyes at the angel in the midst of the light.

"Fear not," said the angel. "For behold I bring you good tidings of great joy, which shall be to all people. For unto you is born this day in the city of David a Saviour, which is Christ the Lord. And this shall be a sign unto you; Ye shall find the babe wrapped in swaddling clothes, lying in a manger."

Suddenly as the shepherds were gazing in wonder, a great throng of angels joined the angel praising God and saying, "Glory to God in the highest, and on earth peace, good will toward men."

Then as the angels returned to heaven and the heavenly music died away, the shepherds began to talk excitedly. "Let us go to Bethlehem, and see this thing that has happened," they said.

Quickly they hurried across the fields to Bethlehem. Most of the people in the village were sleeping, and no twinkling lights welcomed the shepherds.

Coming to a lowly stable, they found Joseph and Mary, and the Babe wrapped in a blanket lying on fresh hay in a manger just as the angel had told them. Joseph and Mary allowed the shepherds to see the precious baby whom they had named Jesus as God had told them before He was born.

Mary listened carefully to what the shepherds told about the angels and their song. She wanted to remember and think about the angels' message.

No doubt it was morning when the shepherds went back out to the streets of Bethlehem, full of joy. They stopped to tell people on the streets the wonderful news of the birth of Jesus and the angels' message.

People were astonished by the story and repeated it to others.

Yes, the shepherds were the very first ones to tell the wonderful story of Jesus. Someone has been telling it ever since. Today the news is as beautiful as ever. That is why I am telling it to you. Will you tell it to someone else?

THE STAR'S SECRET

Long ago in the far East, there lived some men who were very wise. Often at night they went out and looked at the beautiful sky lighted with millions of God's star-lamps. It seemed to them that the stars told them secrets.

One silvery night they did indeed learn a strange secret. A beautiful star was shining which they had never seen before. At once they remembered a story they had heard about a people called the Jews far to the west of them. They believed that some day God would send them a great King from heaven. When the wise men saw this star, they knew this story had come true.

"The King has come!" they exclaimed. "It is the star of the King!"

Then the wise men decided to go and find the King. They loaded their camels with enough food and water to last through the long trip across the great sandy desert. In the evenings after the sun had set, the stars came out one by one. Suddenly they cried out together, "The Star! The star of the King!"

The night was very still and bright when the wise men set out across the desert to find the King. The tall camels cast long shadows over the sands as they strode along. They knew the God of the star was watching over them. They bowed their heads and prayed to Him.

All night they traveled. At last the dawn came stealing gently over the great desert. Then the sun came up, and the day grew warm. They could not travel in the burning heat, so they pitched their tents and rested during the long daytime hours. But as soon as night came on, they folded up their tents and journeyed on.

For many nights the wise men traveled, coming nearer, always nearer to the great King. At last the tall camels stood before the gates of Jerusalem, the great city of the Jews.

The wise men went into the city asking everyone they met, "Where is He that is born King of the Jews? We have seen His star in the East, and are come to worship Him."

The strange story soon reached the ears of King Herod. He was troubled. Who was this King coming to take his throne?

Quickly the king called all the Jewish leaders together, saying, "These strangers from the East speak of a King of the Jews. Tell me, if you know, where is this King to be born?"

"In Bethlehem of Judea, O King," they replied.

Quickly the king sent for the wise men to come to his palace. "Go to Bethlehem," he said, "and you will find this King of the Jews.

And when you have found Him come and tell me. I too, want to worship Him."

The wise men hastened out to the city gates where their camels patiently waited for them. Suddenly, looking up they saw the star hanging low in the sky, like a great golden lamp. It seemed like a friend that had come to show them the way to go. They were filled with great joy.

As the wise men mounted their camels, the star began to move slowly before them. They followed as it led them over the south road toward the little town of Bethlehem. When they reached the town of Bethlehem, the wonderful star stood still, not over a beautiful palace, but directly above a quiet little village home.

The wise men took the rich gifts they had brought and went into the house to find the King. They found Mary with a tiny Child in her arms, and Joseph standing by; but they knew at once that this tiny Child was the King of the Jews. They gave Him their gifts and thanked God for leading them to the King.

That night as the wise men slept, an angel came to them and said, "Do not go back to the king and tell him what you have found. He wants to kill this little Child. Go back to your country by another way." The very next day the wise men set out for their home far away in the East.

Soon afterward, the angel spoke to Joseph one night. "Be quick!" he said, "take the

Child and His mother and go to the land of Egypt, for Herod will try to kill the Child!"

Joseph arose at once and took the young Child and His mother and departed during the night. By morning they were miles on their way.

After a journey of many days and nights the three came to Egypt. There in the land of the pyramids Jesus grew into a happy little boy.

After the wicked king Herod had died the angel again came to Joseph in a dream. "Arise, take the young Child and His mother and go into the land of Israel, for they are dead who wanted to kill Him," he said. And Joseph took his family to a little town called Nazareth where Jesus grew to manhood.

A DRINK OF WATER

Before Jesus was born, God told Joseph to call Him *Jesus* because He would save people from their sins. When Jesus became a man, He went about doing good, helping people, and telling stories that would help them to do right.

One day when Jesus and His helpers, the disciples, had been trudging along a dusty road for many hours, Jesus became tired. He sat down by a well to rest while His friends went to a village to buy food.

Soon a woman carrying a pitcher came to

the well. "Will you please give Me a drink?" asked Jesus.

"What?" exclaimed the woman in surprise. "You are a Jew, and I am a Samaritan. Jews do not like Samaritans. How is it that You asked me for a drink?"

"If you knew who I am," said Jesus, "you would have asked Me for a drink; and I would have given it to you."

"Sir," said the woman, "You have nothing with which to draw water. This well is deep. Then how could You give me water?"

"If you drink water from this well," said Jesus, "you will become thirsty again. But whoever drinks of the water that I have to give will never be thirsty again."

"Sir," said the woman timidly, "give me a drink of that water."

What Jesus meant was that He could take away the sadness from her heart and put a true happiness in its place. It would be much like taking a cold drink of water on a very warm day. But the woman did not understand.

"Go home," said Jesus suddenly, "and call your husband, and come back."

"I have no husband," she said.

"That is true," said Jesus. "You have had five husbands, and the one you now have is not your husband."

"Why!" exclaimed the woman, "You must be a prophet, because You know everything that I ever did."

144

Soon the woman set down her pitcher. Running back to the city she said, "Come see a Man who told me all the things I have ever done!"

Some people followed her back to the well. Jesus was waiting to talk to them. After He had told them many wonderful things, they begged Him to go back to the city with them and tell them more about God. Jesus spent two happy days with them, and many of the people in the city learned to love Him.

"Now," they said to the woman, "we believe in Jesus, not only because of what you told us, but because of the wonderful things we have seen and heard for ourselves. We know that He is indeed the Christ, the Saviour of the world."

THE STORM ON GALILEE

One beautiful evening when no one thought of a storm coming up, Jesus and His disciples were walking along the seashore. If there were children playing along the shore, Jesus probably stopped to talk to them and lay His hand on their heads.

After a while they stepped into a boat and began to row toward the other side of the sea. Jesus often spent the night praying to His Father in heaven, working during the day, healing people who were lame, sick, or blind. Tonight He was tired. He lay down in the bottom of the boat and was soon fast asleep.

Then suddenly, right out of the quiet evening sky, a fierce storm came down upon the Sea of Galilee. The wind blew, and the boat tossed about like an egg shell. It was filling up with water. But still Jesus lay sleeping.

When the boat was about to sink, the disciples woke Jesus saying, "Master, Master, don't You care that we are sinking?"

When Jesus opened His eyes, He saw the frightened faces of the disciples. The angry waves of the rolling sea were dashing into the boat.

Was the Lord Jesus afraid of the dreadful storm? No, He arose and rebuked the wind. He spoke to it above its roaring as if He were speaking to a wild animal to tame it. To the sea He said, "Peace, be still." Instantly the wind and the raging water grew quiet. There was a great calm.

The waters were smooth and the boat rocked gently once more. Then Jesus asked His disciples, "Why are you so fearful? How is it that you have no faith?"

They looked from one to the other asking, "What kind of a man is this that even the winds and the sea obey Him?" Although they could not understand the wonderfulness of their Master, they were glad to be out on the sea with Him after the storm.

WHEN ZACCHAEUS
MET JESUS

Zacchaeus was a rich man who had never seen Jesus. When he heard that Jesus was passing through Jericho, the town where he lived, Zacchaeus was determined to see him.

This short, energetic little man pushed and shoved to get through the great crowd that was with Jesus. It was no use. There were so many people he couldn't get close. Then Zacchaeus got an idea. He ran ahead of the great crowd and climbed up into a sycamore tree. There he looked down on the crowd.

Yes, Jesus was coming! He was walking along the dusty road and talking very earnestly to the people He loved. Zacchaeus watched His every move as He came closer.

When Jesus reached the tree, He stood still. He looked up into the tree, and everybody heard Him calling in a clear voice, "Zacchaeus, hurry up and come down. Today I must stay at your house."

Quickly Zacchaeus swung himself down to the ground, all smiles. "Come," he exclaimed joyfully.

The crowd parted, and the two went off together, with Jesus' close friends following. There was a murmuring in the crowd as they passed. "What a man for Jesus of Nazareth to visit!" they whispered. "That tax gatherer, Zacchaeus, has cheated many poor people out of their hard-earned money. If he were an honest man, he would not be so rich!"

Zacchaeus took Jesus to his beautiful home, where Jesus talked earnestly to the tax collector. Never before had Zacchaeus met such a man as Jesus Christ. In a short time a very wonderful thing happened to him. The selfishness went out of his heart and a love for God took its place. He began to love people. He became a new man!

Suddenly Zacchaeus stood to his feet and said, "Lord, I will give half of my money to the poor. And if I have taken anything that belonged to other people I will give back four times as much as I took."

His face was beaming with happiness. Jesus, too, was happy as He replied, "Today salvation has come to this house. Now you can understand why I came into this world. It was to look for men who have been lost away from God, as you have been, to find them and bring them back."

That was the happiest day the little man had ever known. Jesus Christ soon went on His way, but Zacchaeus remembered his promise. Can you imagine how surprised the people were when this once selfish man began to give money to the poor? Can you imagine how happy the poor people he had cheated were to have returned to them four times as much as he had taken?

Now Zacchaeus was no longer hated by the people. He had become a friend of the poor.

JAIRUS' LITTLE DAUGHTER

Jairus and his wife loved their only daughter very dearly. When she was twelve years old, she became very ill. In spite of everything that her parents did it seemed that she would die.

At last Jairus went to find Jesus and ask Him to help them. Finding Him in the midst of a great throng of people, he fell at His feet crying, "My little daughter is at the point of death. I pray Thee to come and lay hands on her so she may be healed."

When Jesus arose and followed him, many people thronged after Him. The crowd was so large they pushed against each other. After a while one of Jairus' servants came through the crowd. "Your daughter is dead. Do not bother the Master anymore," he said.

When Jesus heard these words, he turned to Jairus and said, "Do not be afraid. Only believe and she shall be made whole."

When they came to the home of Jairus, many people were there weeping and wailing. "Why do you make all this noise and weep?" asked Jesus. "The little girl is not dead. She is sleeping."

The crowd of people laughed at Him because they knew the child was dead. Jesus sent them all out. Then taking the child's parents and two of His disciples, Peter and

John, He went into the room where the little girl lay and closed the door.

He took the little girl by the hand and said gently, "Little girl, arise!" And immediately she arose and walked. The people were all astonished. Jesus instructed them not to tell what had happened and told them to give the child something to eat.

How happy the little girl's father and mother were to have her alive and well once more!

THE WIDOW'S GIFT

A long time ago there were some wise men who studied the Bible so much they almost knew it by heart. They copied parts of it on scrolls so other people could read it. These men were called scribes.

Although these men read the Bible so much, they did not do some of the things it told them to do. To be sure, they loved to make people think they were good men. Everyone looked at them admiringly when they came out on the street dressed in their long robes with fringes around the bottom. Sometimes when they came to the street corners where many people were passing, they stopped and made long prayers. They wanted everybody to see them praying.

But in their hearts these scribes were very selfish and wicked. Jesus knew this, because He could look into their minds and see what they were thinking. Their selfishness showed too, in the things they did. God tells us in the Bible that we should help the widows and orphans. These men had often read this in the Bible, but they did not do it.

One day Jesus was in the temple talking to these proud scribes. They were listening angrily. While He talked, the people were coming up to the offering boxes and dropping in their gifts of money for the Lord. Some held their heads high, for they were bringing generous gifts.

Then a poor woman came up timidly. She was afraid that somebody would see her and notice how little she had. She did not see Jesus watching her. She dropped in two little pieces of money and quietly slipped away.

By this time a crowd of people had gathered around Jesus. He said to them, "This poor widow has given more than you all. I have been watching you bring your gifts. Some of you have given much, but you have plenty of money left at home. But this woman has given to God all that she had."

The poor woman went home. In her heart she knew she had done right, and she was happy.

WHEN JESUS DIED

It is hard to believe that someone as kind, loving, and helpful as the Lord Jesus Christ would have any enemies. But there were some people who hated Him. They refused to believe the message the angel had given to the shepherds when Jesus was born and laid in a manger. They did not believe He was the Son of God. They found fault with everything He did. At last their hatred grew so bitter they determined to kill Him.

It was late, and the city of Jerusalem was fast asleep when the soldiers led Jesus through the streets. They took Him to the palace of the high priest.

A crowd of rough people quickly gathered about Jesus. They played a cruel and wicked game. Blindfolding Him, they struck Him on the face saying roughly, "Tell us who struck You, Prophet!"

When morning came at last, they took Jesus to the palace of Pilate the governor. "We want Him to be crucified," they said.

Pilate asked Jesus some questions. Then turning to the crowd he said quietly, "I find no fault in Him. He has done nothing wrong."

But the crowd was angry and determined, "Crucify Him! Crucify Him!" they cried fiercely.

When Pilate saw he could not change their minds, he called for a basin of water. Washing his hands slowly, he said, "I am free from the blame of this. You may crucify Him if you wish. But, remember, you are to blame."

Soon a great crowd of people was flocking through the streets toward the city gates. In the midst of the crowd walked Jesus, carrying a heavy wooden cross they had placed on His back. He had had no rest the night before. His back was sore from the beating they had given Him during the night. At last He could go no further. Then they called to a man who was passing by, and made him carry the cross the rest of the way.

At last they came to a hill called Calvary, outside the city. Here they laid the cross on the ground and fastened Jesus to it by driving nails through His hands and His feet.

Then lifting up the cross they stood back to watch Jesus die. His mother and His best friend John stood close by.

Looking down at His mother, Jesus spoke to her lovingly. To John he said, "Behold your mother." From that time on John took Mary, the mother of Jesus, to his home as though she were his own mother.

There were two other crosses on the hilltop. On these crosses, one on either side of Jesus, the soldiers had nailed two thieves. One of them turned his head toward Jesus, "Why don't You save Yourself and us from this terrible death?" he asked angrily.

"Do not speak to Him so," said the other thief gently. "We are dying because we are wicked men and deserve to die. But this Man has never done anything wrong." And to Jesus he said, "Lord, remember me when You come into Your kingdom."

"Today," Jesus answered him, "you shall be with Me in Paradise."

Although it was noontime, the world grew as dark as night. The great throng of people became strangely quiet. Suddenly the voice of the dying Jesus rang out over the hillside, "It is finished!" and He bowed His head and died. At the same moment there was a great roar, and the earth trembled and shook. A Roman soldier standing by the cross of Jesus with bowed head, said, "Truly this Man was the Son of God."

In the evening two men asked Pilate if they might take down the body of Jesus and bury it. These men had been followers of Jesus and loved Him for a long time, but they had been afraid to let people know about it. One was Joseph, a good and wise man. The other man was Nicodemus, who had long before come to talk to Jesus at night.

Gently they laid the body of Jesus into a tomb that had been cut out of solid rock, in a beautiful garden. It was Joseph's own tomb in which he had himself expected to be buried sometime. But he wanted Jesus' body to rest in this lovely spot.

Soon rough, rude soldiers came to watch by the tomb, so the friends of Jesus could not come and steal His body. And so at last the night came, the night of the saddest day in all the world.

JESUS LIVING AGAIN

The body of Jesus lay quietly, undisturbed in the tomb. Outside, birds sang sweetly, but all was quiet in the tomb.

Very early on Sunday morning the soldiers sat in the garden nodding and dozing. Suddenly a deep rumbling in the earth beneath their feet startled them. It was an earthquake! There was a flash like lightning, and a white-robed angel came down from heaven. The soldiers were terrified. They trembled, shook, and became as dead men. When they opened their eyes again, the heavy stone door of the tomb was pushed away and stood wide open!

Soon three women came walking softly into the garden. They were bringing spices and perfumes to make the body of Jesus sweet and fragrant. One whispered to another, "Who will roll away the stone for us?"

As they came nearer, they stopped and looked at one another in astonishment. The stone was rolled away!

Mary Magdalene turned and ran swiftly back to the city. "They have taken away my

Lord out of the tomb, and we know not where they have laid Him!" she panted.

The other women stooped down and went into the tomb. Two shining angels were there. "Why do you look for Jesus here?" they asked. "He is not here. He is risen!"

After the others were gone, Mary Magdalene came back to the garden. She stood outside the tomb crying. Then she stooped and looked inside. The tomb was flooded with light, for the angels were still there.

"Woman," said the angels, "why do you weep?"

"Because they have taken away my Lord, and I know not where they have laid Him," she sobbed.

As she turned and walked in the garden, Someone stood beside her. "Woman," He said gently, "why do you weep?"

"Oh, Sir," she cried, "if you have taken Him away, tell me where you have laid Him!"

"Mary!" said He.

She looked up quickly. "Master!" she cried.

"Yes," said Jesus. "It is I. Go and tell My friends that I am alive again, and that I am going back to God."

Later that day two sad-faced men were walking along a country road, when a Stranger came up behind them. "What are you talking about, and why are you so sad?" He asked kindly.

"Are You a stranger in these parts?" they

asked. "Do You not know what has happened?"

"What?" asked the Man.

"There was a great prophet among us, named Jesus," explained the two men. "We had hoped He was the Redeemer God has promised to send from heaven. But now He is dead."

The Stranger walked on down the road with them, talking as He went. When they came near to the village where they were going, they said to Him, "It is evening now. Come and stay with us tonight." So they all went together into a quiet home.

After praying, the Stranger took the food and passed it to the men. Instantly they knew He was Jesus! They started to speak. They seemed to have a hundred things to tell Him. But suddenly His seat was empty. He was gone!

Forgetting how tired they were, the two men started to walk the seven long miles back to Jerusalem. There they found their friends all talking together excitedly. Suddenly Jesus Himself stood among them and said, "Peace."

They were very frightened, but Jesus said, "Look at My hands and feet, where the nails were driven. See, it is I, Jesus."

He told them He was going away, but He would send the Holy Spirit to be with them. They would not be able to see Him, but they would feel Him in their hearts.

One day, Jesus walked out to Mount Olivet

with His best friends. When they reached the mountain top, He lifted up His hands, blessed them, and spoke a few last, loving words. Then, while they were watching, He began slowly to rise up toward the blue sky. Up, up, up He went, until a fleecy cloud hid Him from their sight.

At that instant two men stood by His friends. "Men of Galilee," they said, "why do you stand gazing up into heaven? This same Jesus will come again in the same way you have seen Him go into heaven."

Then the friends of Jesus went back to Jerusalem to pray and happily wait for the promise Jesus gave of the coming of His Holy Spirit.